In Search of Purpose

In Search *of* Purpose

Ola Barnabas

PARTRIDGE

Scripture quotations marked KJV are from the Holy Bible, King James Version (Authorized Version). First published in 1611. Quoted from the KJV Classic Reference Bible, Copyright © 1983 by The Zondervan Corporation.

Scripture quotations marked AMP are from *The Amplified Bible*, Old Testament copyright © 1965, 1987 by the Zondervan Corporation. *The Amplified Bible*, New Testament copyright © 1954, 1958, 1987 by The Lockman Foundation. Used by permission. All rights reserved.

Unless otherwise indicated, all scripture quotations are from *The Holy Bible, English Standard Version® (ESV®)*. Copyright ©2001 by Crossway Bibles, a division of Good News Publishers. Used by permission. All rights reserved.

Scripture quotations marked NIV are taken from the *Holy Bible, New International Version®. NIV®.* Copyright © 1973, 1978, 1984 by International Bible Society. Used by permission of Zondervan. All rights reserved. [Biblica]

Print information available on the last page.

To order additional copies of this book, contact
Toll Free 0800 990 914 (South Africa)
+44 20 3014 3997 (outside South Africa)
orders.africa@partridgepublishing.com

www.partridgepublishing.com/africa

Contents

Dedication

To the Creator who made us all with definite purpose in mind

To the people who helped me find mine

To you who is searching

Acknowledgement

No way. There is just no way a book like this is written without the input of several people usually whose names the writer may omit. Usually I would skip this part so I don't make the mistake, but my publisher would have none of that. I apologize in advance if I do not remember to mention your name. You mean more to me than your name listed here could imply.

God deserves all praise for such a work as this.

My dad laid the foundation for my journey to personal discovery. The insight he has about the lives of all his children, the faith he had in me, and the way he guided me through, even in death, I am forever grateful to him. My mum has continued to carry on the great job that was started. A soon-to-be great grand mum, a woman who lives practically on her knees before God, a pride inestimable.

My wife and son, they pay the highest price always. I travel a lot to speak, train, do business and all that, and when I'm at home, I sit in the desk for hours writing, thinking, planning and doing all these kinds of things more than I'm willing to admit. Thank you dearies, I love you more every day.

The family of God like I would like to describe them – the carriers of His grace, men who played and are still playing their part in shaping the lives that have been committed to their care of whom I am lucky to be one – Rev. George Adegboye, Pastors Victor and Christiana Akure, Toyin Bello and Jacob Ajakaiye, I am grateful. Pastors N.O. Awojide, Chris Itseumah, Gabriel Obaseki, Albert Oduwole, Godwin Ogwuche, Oyerinde Adeniyi, Prof. Steve Arogbonlo, Dr Osita Abia, and all members of this great family, thank you.

Philip John, Emily, Divine and all team members at Partridge Publishing Africa, thanks for taking the pain to follow me up. To the Sanjane Publication team members, it is your combined efforts that made this a success.

To all friends of mine, too many to mention, all influencers, mentees, teens and all, thank you so much for helping me to improve.

Preface

The search for purpose is a search that everyone engages in. To be emphatic, we search every day in the things that we do, the questions we ask, the observations we make, the things we are interested in, the people we associate with, the places we go, and even the books that we read. Our lives' purpose is not for us to determine, it is for us to discover, thus the search.

This search is spiritual. Its cavernous-ness is in answering the train of a string of questions: Is there a God? Is He the One who created us? Will the Creator make someone (something) without a purpose for him (it)? Can the creation understand why he (it) was created without referring to the Creator? Can the creation even understand why he was even created? Could the search for purpose become easier if the creation follows the lead of the Creator?

There are other parameters that are considered in this book that could lead towards the discovery of purpose. Parameters within the realm of human reasoning and understanding.

In Search of Purpose is therefore a fusion of both spiritual and human reasoning. The perspicacity of the search made this fusion imperative. The themes examined are broad, the context engaging, the submissions sizzling yet the language simple.

The search for one's purpose is sometimes quizzical. Sometimes we think we know what our purpose is, sometimes we doubt if we know. Sometimes we think what we are doing couldn't be described else. That must be our purpose. But some of these times we really couldn't be farther from fulfilling that purpose. Sometimes we beat our chest in confidence that what we are doing is what we are in the world to do, and sometimes we just ask ourselves: "How do you know?"

Reminds me of a story I once read. A Chinese farmer once had a horse that ran away. Neighbours gathered to sympathize with him, and they said: "That is too bad". He shrugged his shoulders and asked, "How do you know?" The next day the horse returned with several other wild horses to the house. The neighbors gathered again, this time, to celebrate with the man and they said: "That is so great". The man shrugged his shoulders again and replied them, "How do you know?" The following day, his son was dressing the horses and one of the horses kicked him and he broke his leg. The neighbors came to sympathize with him and they said: "That is too bad". Once again the man shrugged his shoulders and replied them, "How do you know?" The following day, the king sent that all young boys in the village be drafted for war in the northern part of the country, and the boy couldn't be drafted. You know what's coming next right? The neighbors gathered again and… and so the story continued.

Sometimes we go through good, sometimes bad. Sometimes we try implementing an idea hoping it works, sometimes we don't even want to try. Sometimes we choose a career path hoping that's the best for us. Sometimes we make up our minds on someone and choose to marry them instead of someone else that's equally qualified for our love. Reminds me further of someone's diary I'd seen sometimes ago, and I read a page in it where he wrote: "Love is such a mystery. It's confusing yet effusing. It's such a silly thing that beats my imagination. I've seen people who love me, I mean ladies who will do anything to keep me. I've loved one, maybe two persons before and truly desired a life with them. Something, somehow just sometimes happens that makes neither their dream nor mine come through. Granted, you can't end up with everyone you love in life, at best you can only marry one of them especially if you are a Christian. But what exactly happens when the man or lady you love the most is unfortunately married?

Or what do you do when you are unfortunately married but there's someone you would rather have got married to, especially if that other person loves you just as much? Do you fight for love or just let it go? Does the fact of someone's marriage negate or obliterate the love they once had and truly still do have for another person?"

Life is really just a composite of 'could have beens' and 'sometimes'. The path of life is filled with 'sometimes'. What we consider 'bad' might not really be bad after all. What we thought 'good' might turn out to be not so good after all, but like the old farmer asks, how do you know?

In ten chapters, the job is done or is rather just beginning, because the reading of this text is only a part of the job. And I hope that you will not only read but study this text, apply the lessons and ultimately, I hope that this text helps you in the search for your purpose.

Introduction

Early in the year two thousand and eight it was, about a year after my first academic book was published. Everything that could possibly go wrong had gone wrong with me. I guess what they call Murphy's Law had finally caught up with me and had even overtaken me. I was in dire straits by all measures – financially, emotionally, spiritually, physically and all the …llys. I found myself in Kano, Nigeria, seeking asylum, literally, and to redefine my life.

I don't know if you have gone through that time yet in your life. A time that you wish never shows up in your life. For some people it is as short as weeks, some people months, others like myself years. Times when the companion you are sure to have every night is sorrow. You are locked up inside with deep- seated emotions and pain that nobody, in every sense of that word understands. Every time you try to explain, you are saying one thing, what they are hearing is different, and you wonder if it is not really better to spare everyone a further explanation. And when they ask you, you just reply "it is well" when that statement is more a wish for you than an experience.

Mine was not so short a time. For whatever reason, I groped in the wilderness of life for far longer than I'd love to admit. I cannot really say this or that year was when it all started but it was just like a joke, and then it got out of hand. I'll spare you the real details; it's all a compound of rhetoric. But there is a part that concerns the theme of this book, and which I hope helps someone.

Everyone tried to help me. The church I attended – a beautiful church for all purposes and intents, wonderful pastors who wanted nothing but the best, tried as hard as they could, not many of them really connected with me. They tried to create an opening for me so I could get my hands busy and at least get something to keep body and soul together. At another time, I was literally forced to go attend an interview for a teaching job at a school. I've never felt worse in my life coming back from that interview. I was called to pick up the job in the school, but the thought of it alone was enough punishment in my soul.

I know there you are reading this page, and everyone looks like they are doing everything they really could do to help, and it may even appear to them like you are not willing to be helped. This here is to tell you that you are not alone. You've got to remind yourself of what you are sure God told you if you heard Him. No one was there when you heard Him. No one can possibly understand what only you heard. Try hard they may, but give you a direction they can't. It is the vision that He planted in you that drives your life. You may be struggling with the understanding of it, or the fulfillment of it, or both. The people in your life who are trying to show you love also are struggling to understand. The difference is, while you are struggling to understand the purpose of your being, they are trying to understand what is going on with you. One looks on from the inside, the other from the outside. Both are struggling. Except a matured soul among them or one who's had a similar experience finds a way of connecting with you, or you find a way of letting them in on your incontinence, you may never be able to receive their love, and you will only keep telling them "You don't understand". The search for purpose can really be unsettling.

I resolved eventually to abandon myself to service in my local church. I would go to the church office, and use my management knowledge and experience from other bigger churches that I'd been in, to help set up a functioning system in the church. I'd resume like I would at a normal place of work, and close as appropriate. I formed closer bond and relationship with the pastor and his wife and we talked a lot at times, discussions that filled the void of loneliness that was traumatizing my very soul at the time. I would return home to the company of my friends whose generosity I would never forget. These were people who made sure I smiled every day before bed even when I had no reason to.

Then the inevitable happened.

I had become so useful for the church, it was thought of me to become a staff – an administrative officer. An honor to me I must say. I could perhaps be the first to have been considered for such a role apart from a youth Corp member who had served with the church while I volunteered. I didn't take the job.

Maybe I was considered as someone who didn't want to be helped, or as one who thought he knew everything but was obviously stuck on the road to progress, or so it felt to me. If you are thinking I was lazy that's why I didn't want to work, that's not correct. That was not the reason I was volunteering. I've always known volunteering is what I should do in my Father's house, and besides, it was a 'get-away from me-self' time. The job provided the perfect hiding place for me from myself, and that was all I wanted, there was nothing I wanted more. Further, I didn't want the money to become a defining factor for the priceless relationship I had built. It was on the basis of these reasons that I declined the job.

Above all these, there was a stirring up inside of me. Purpose was calling and the decibels of the sound of that call was deafening. Only I could hear it. It was my purpose.

I had started on the track to my purpose fulfillment more consciously some ten years before or earlier. Even though I will not claim that I would have been able to state categorically that this and this is who I am or why I am created, I was at least moving in the direction of what I loved to do which is not far from what I do today. Purpose was already being formed in me, I was already pursuing it. The God-incidence that set me on the path of purpose would unsettle me as long as I would not do what I should be doing. That led me to hide from myself.

So, the quest for my purpose left no joy in me whenever options came up that were not in tandem with my purpose, not even taking up church administrative work could fill that void. I struggled so badly, and I guess I really suck at struggling, that every well-intended alternative was badly taken. That I think goes for you too who has found yourself in an inconsolable corner of life. People reach out to you with good intentions, but because their good intentions do not answer the questions of your life, you just hope they stop trying, and just let you be; maybe soon you will get over it. But because they love you, they won't go away from you, and that I think is probably one time in life when love hurts.

The struggle and pain sealed up inside you are truly inexplicable to others. Not many understand from your point of view. The voice you are responding to is that of purpose. The unease you feel is the stirring of purpose. Ask women who are led into the delivery room, and they will confirm to you how easy or not it is for them, at least, until the baby comes out. Purpose is a baby that will not let you rest until you birth it. That labour pang may have been triggered by your unemployment, tiredness with your current job, indebtedness or financial inadequacy, lack of family, lack of support from anyone, natural dissatisfaction, feeling of disadvantaged position in life, etc. whatever the trigger is, I feel for you, even though all I'm offering now is just words. I only hope that you are able to get the strength to push through at the right time and birth your purpose for living.

And here I am writing these words to you, and taking a glance at the burgeoning tummy my wife has on her in which my child is being incubated. I really just wonder how it feels in there, both for him and the mother. I know the day will come when he will be born, will grow up, and also set to searching for his purpose in life. He will probably be asking me what I think he should do with his life, what decision I think is best for him, probably thinking his father is an expert on these matters. I have an answer before the question is posed. It is like I would say unto you too in the course of this book. This search is your search, this pursuit is your take, the discovery is yours to make; but search, all the same, pursue because your life depends on it.

The pursuit of purpose is the pursuit of happiness, and like most such endeavors, there is happiness in the pursuit. I assure you, very few people engage in the search for the ultimate purpose for which they are alive, and so fewer number get to live truly fulfilling lives. You are out on that journey, and I do hope you travel all the way till you find what you are looking for, and not give up the search. The search is worth it.

1

The Purpose Me

WHAT PURPOSE IS

I had gone in and out of the rooms about four times, couldn't tell if I was just pacing or if I was looking for anything, I honestly didn't know what it was. I became tired of the rounds that I eventually shouted at myself: What on earth am I in this room for?! I needed to know what my purpose in the room was, and I had just no clue. Eventually, I got out... with nothing, because I could not even know it or tell if I saw what I was looking for.

Life could just be a charade many a time, a soccer game without goal posts, a race without the finish line, a ridiculous hallucination of intentions, a dire 'What am I here for?!' strait. Purpose, when not discovered early, shows up in what is regarded as the mid-life crisis, and when not resolved still, shows up on the death bed as life's regrets. The decibel of purpose increases per unit as we grow through life. While we spend the early part of our life searching out what exactly we want to do with our lives, and trying to fix ourselves in one thing or the other that we consider that we are fit for, and while we keep failing, falling and trying, we just go through the struggles of trying to hear that sound and truly wish somebody could just tell us and save us the stress. As we approach mid-life, we tend to see somehow what we are created for, but we may have got ourselves into so many things that just get us by. Like our routine jobs. Even though they are boring, and we just dread every Monday, we dread also the thought of leaving those jobs or any other thing for that matter to pursue what we think we are created for. After all, it is important that we are able to keep body and soul together, and take care of the bills. *Abi*? I think it's really a shame that our jobs replace our purpose.

Some people don't even discover or see a reflection of their purpose in mid-life. Many discover their life's purpose on their death bed, for those who have the opportunity to be there when it happens. I hear that people hardly do not know why they have been created on their death beds. The units of the decibels are so high that people just know what really mattered to them. It's not a stramash anymore; it's a clearly distinctive sound of regret. You know regret is a sound of something you know you should have done that you didn't do. How sorry-full to hear dying people wish they had done this or that.

We are all at one point or another of discovering what next to do with our lives. This search is what really makes life interesting. If we just knew it, life would be so boring. If you are searching at this time for "Who am I?" "Why am I here?" "Where am I going?" it is a big congratulation to you because you are making the search that matters the most.

The Encarta dictionaries define purpose as the reason for which something exists, has been done or made; the goal or intended outcome of something; the desire or the resolve necessary to accomplish a goal. Most dictionaries agree with the definition given: the reason for which something (someone) has been done or made – the purpose of life.

It was the iconic Myles Munroe who once said: "When purpose is not discovered, abuse is inevitable." How exactly do we live without knowing what we are to live for? Purpose is the very thing that defines our existence, the non-discovery of which makes for a very miserable life. The search for purpose is the search for which man is created. There goes the saying: If a man does not know where he is going, everywhere looks like it. Mark Twain once said, "The two most important days in your life are the day you are born and the day you find out why." My friend, your purpose is your palace. When you discover why you are created and you set about achieving it, you sit and reign as a king in that palace and you set yourself up for greatness. You set yourself up for fulfillment in life.

The ultimate success in life is in becoming that for which you are created. Everyone is created for something and everyone has the potential to discover why they are created. Are you searching? Well, that you are reading this book answers that question in a way, but you know as well as I do that it doesn't end here.

We can, you and I can travel the mile in search of why you are here if you stick it out with me in this book, digest and apply the lessons, tests, principles and all herein. But we can only go so far. The search for purpose is farther than a mile, is farther than one great book can take you. You can, and will be set on the path with this book, the ultimate search, however, is a life-long journey. As you succeed on a road, I assure you, you will get to another junction in life where you are still asking the question: What next now? We all do.

PURPOSE DEFINED

As in many cases, there are many synonyms to describe a concept. I checked up the Latin words for Purpose in several dictionaries and this is what I got: animus, consilium, finis, inductio, institutum, ipsum, propositum, sententia, voluntas.

Let's examine the meaning/synonyms of some of these words:

- **consilium:** policy, advice, counsel, arrangement, council, reason, purpose, wisdom

- **finis:** limit, border, boundary, end, close, extent, goal, stop, summit, territory, ultimate point

- **inductio:** induction, leading in, application, bringing in, inclination, intention, resolution

- **institutum:** plan, custom, established law, institute, institution, way of life, principle, purpose

- **propositum:** purpose, aim, design, plan, program, project, thesis

- **sententia:** sentence, assertion, view, decision, judgment, maxim, purpose, motto, opinion, will

- **voluntas:** choice, desire, inclination, disposition, purpose, will, wish

There's quite coverage with those synonyms that describe purpose. finis actually describes it as the close; the ultimate point. In other words, there is no further going from here. Quite interesting! propositum describes it as a design; a plan; a thesis. My addition: a divine design of man's life. These are beyond mere words. sententia describes it as a motto. One's purpose is the slogan for his life! That's beyond amazing. Using the first two above, we could describe man's purpose as: **A divine design of a man's life - his ultimate reason for living**.

THE QUEST FOR PURPOSE

Everyone is created for a purpose. There is no manufacturer who just makes a product for the sake of it. Humans are products of a divine Creator and were created because of specific purposes that the Creator wants to be accomplished. While some people's purposes are clearly unique, some others share very similar purpose with other creatures and are very much likely to succeed working among people of similar purpose as theirs. In the final analysis, though, all our purposes wind up to the ultimate purpose in the heart of the Creator. We all play our little roles in that ultimate purpose.

Sadly, however, very few people truly discover their real purpose before death. As a matter of fact, methinks some of the leading causes of death are such causes relating to unfulfilled life, undiscovered life, life without meaning and lacking in drive, and there is no way these issues are rested except that purpose is discovered.

In *The Path to Purpose: Helping Our Children Find Their Calling in Life*, William Damon showed by research that only 20 percent of youth age 12 to 26 had found something meaningful that they wanted to dedicate their lives to. 25 percent of youth were "drifting," in want of a wider purpose, or not even making plans to find one, and others are just somewhere in between.

Many people are rather pre-occupied with meeting everyday personal and family needs and living from hand to mouth so badly that they age through time but feel a great disconnect between what they are doing, and what they think their life is about. At its worst, such people just numb out on life and accept the hideous unfulfilled life that they have as their cross or destiny as some people call it. They call it fate too. They redefine their destiny to be what they have boxed it to become. They limit their fates to meeting their daily needs. They take the path of convenience by blaming some fate or life for handing them what they have. On the contrary, we all are responsible for our choices in life. Our lives are what we created or recreated it to be.

The greatest curse with living without purpose is, not knowing that there is one to start with. Only those who know they have a purpose can even make efforts to discover it. You may never look for anything if you did not know you lost it. This is foundational, and so is the error of not knowing it. If we can just know that there is such a thing called purpose that we are in this world to achieve, then we will, maybe, set out to find what that purpose could possibly be.

If you find the Purpose you are searching for, will you know it?

Search is infinite without a definition. Einstein was said to be on a train and misplaced his ticket while on transit. He bent down and searched everywhere, under the seat, in his pockets, everywhere. He didn't find it, but he didn't stop searching. The attention of the train attendant was called, and he promised Einstein that he didn't need to worry so much about the ticket after all he is the well-known Albert Einstein, but he wouldn't budge. He searched still. When pressed further, he replied: It's not about the ticket, it is the fact that I don't know where I'm going, and the address is on the ticket. Sometimes, we are at sea as it concerns what we really want, some other times, we cannot even tell whether we have found what we are looking for or not.

IT TAKES A FIGHT

Understanding that there is such a thing as purpose and discovering what it is comes differently to all of us. Of course, life turns different sides to us all. So, while Joe found teaching – impacting knowledge as his life's purpose at 18, Bill may live to be 50, and is yet confused as to what he should do with his life. And quite a number of factors could be responsible for this.

Joe may have been born into a home with parents who have deep understanding of these things and were able to guide him early into living out his life the way it ought to be, while Bill grew up almost independently lacking any kind of parental tutelage or had parents who knew little or nothing about what purpose means.

Joe may have been exposed to certain materials – books, mentors, leaders, call it whatever, that helped guide his mind as he grew, in fact, he may have grown up to find that his life is patterned after a particular person, and he just lives by observing the footsteps of that person. Bill, on the other hand, may not have had access to the kind of resources available to Joe. He may have grown up in the traditional manner common with most kids.

The kind of education available to Joe and Bill in their formative years could also be the difference maker, the physical environment into which they grew could be the difference maker, the peers they grew up with could influence them (we'll talk more on this later in the book). Many a time it may even have nothing to do with any physical factors like we have mentioned above, Joe may just have grown up into his purpose. And none of us has full understanding of how that really happens but we know it does. Someone grows up and tends towards some particular activities, profession, interests, etc. and another just grows up lacking a clear direction in which to head.

For both Joe and Bill, they get to know they have a purpose in life and discovering that purpose comes at different prices. Sometimes things don't come just because we wish they did. Most times it takes a fight – I mean a real battle to get down to knowing "What on earth am I here for?"

It is no mean blessing that a youth can define his purpose, and begin to pattern his life after that purpose because there is no better time to know one's purpose than as a youth. It saves a cup- full of tears. The ages between 15 and 25 are so critical to laying the foundation for venturing out at about the age of 30. Reading through the scriptures, you'll find that this age description fits the lives of Joseph the son of Jacob, John the Baptist and even Jesus Christ. Maybe you are reading and thinking about this right now because of your age range and experience and you are shrugging your shoulders and asking like the farmer, "How do you know?" The truth is I really don't and I do not have the authority to set the template for other people's lives, but we all can at least turn to the perfect example in the good book. Discovering purpose at any age is always so sweet. When one discovers it a little late in life, it is valued like a lost treasure, but I assure you that, much more could be accomplished in life, and greater fulfillment had if it is discovered early.

Bill, as well as most of us, has got a battle to fight. There's got to be some digging, asking, searching, thinking, praying, etc, to get to the root of whatever that elusive purpose might be. I mean if you misplace a treasure, you'd look for it frantically anyway, and believe me, there is no treasure greater than purpose.

Whoever cannot answer the question of purpose, cannot answer the question of life. Purpose is identity. A known purpose is the guiding light of any man's life. When a man finds his purpose, there is a surge of electricity, a powering of that light. Something clicks in the spirit of that man that sends life through his mortal body. When purpose is discovered, man's mortality becomes the least of his worries. Ingvar Kamprad of IKEA furniture once said, "I am too busy, I don't have time for dying." If death or the thought of it can no longer keep a man down, what exactly will? That elucidates the impact of purpose discovery. A man finds what his life is about, and he commits his living to it. Nothing keeps a man more alive.

Purpose is the light that illuminates the darkness of life, and there are dark times in life. Times when understanding seems to take a back seat, times when conventional wisdom become grossly inadequate, times when everything one does look like the next foolish decision. Those times are the wilderness of life, and we all go through them every once in a while.

If you find someone at that spot right now, or if you are at that spot in your life, it may not be for any particular fault of theirs or yours. They may not have offended the gods or transgressed beyond pardon. That they do not have answers to the questions of their lives may not be something they are particularly responsible for. It may just be that they are in the wilderness; they are simply going through an experience that is hardly simple. Least you could do, pray with them. To help them further, help them keep in constant view the purpose that lies ahead of them, whether they know it or not, there is hardly a greater help you could render them.

Purpose gives hope, and hope makes alive. You could possibly survive another day of starvation if someone told you there is a meal at the end of the day. The hope that that meal brings keeps you going.

Have you found a man living without purpose? You have found a man who's wasting. If you find a man going nowhere, please tell him he'll get there. If visionlessness kills, and focuslessness keeps in danger of darkness, then what do you think purposelessness does? My friend, get vision, get focus, but with all thy getting, get purpose also for it will keep you alive. Your vision and your focus must be on the very reason for which you are on earth. So fight to find it like he who has lost irreplaceable treasures. Fight to find it, and when you do, fight to become it.

There is something that becoming purpose, and fulfilling it does to you that words are inadequate to describe. It is far beyond ornament and adornment you can count on, it is far beyond the fragrance of costly elements from the Agar wood in the middle east, it is beyond the luxurious lush of a blossoming garden, far beyond the pleasure of a chauffeur-driven posh, it is beyond the knowledge of avalanche of inherited cash reserves, it is far beyond the blessings of good friends and family, far beyond the blessedness of water cascading your body in scorching heat, not even the fantasy of a newly-wed bride can compare. Matter of fact, it creates these things.

When a man finds fulfillment in the life that he has, he bothers less that he does not have these things in the measure that people expect, and quite frankly, I have yet to meet a fulfilled man who lacks these other things. This book is about helping you find that fulfillment, but the discovery cannot be made without you.

HELP, I'M OLD, CAN I STILL FULFILL PURPOSE?

Okay. I admit. I truly won't be able to compare your life as an aged person seeking to discover purpose with that of a youth who has discovered his. But I'd rather that you spend the remaining days of your life living the real you that you were meant to be than continuing in falsehood until you are hosted in the great beyond.

Everyone deserves to be happy in their lives. There is no greater time when one desires to sleep happy than in old age. My dad, of blessed memory, will always say if you find a man who in old age is still breaking firewood for a living, ask what he did with his youth. The old age which represents the night time of one's life actually represents rest time. The good word says the day is given to man to work, and the night time to rest, but many old people have purpose calling out to be fulfilled in them like God called out to Joshua even in old age. He acknowledged "you are old and well-stricken in age" but then added, "but there are more lands to be conquered."

Joshua represents a perfect example of one who has truly worked. I mean except you didn't read the scriptures. You will find that Moses had a great successor in Joshua but fulfillment as far as destiny cries denote a two-fold performance:

- Are you doing what you ought to be doing? The works you are pre-occupied with, are they the works you should really be doing?

- If they are, have you been doing enough? Because to every man, there is an apportionment. Unto one He gave one, to another two, and yet another five. The One who created us for a purpose also infused us with strength for the delivery of the purpose according to His expectation of us.

It is no doubt that Joshua passed the first performance criteria, and probably thought he was doing well with the second, but, not so God. As revealed in the word, Joshua didn't do enough. That is probably your state now too. You got to go beyond you are doing. You got to go beyond measuring how well you are doing by the standards of people – they did not commission you on that purpose you are pursuing, God did. You got to go beyond measuring how well you are doing by your own standards, you are not of yourself, you are God's. You can only correctly measure yourself by the standards that He has set for you. It's got to be only by His standard, that, and that alone. That's when you'll know whether you are doing what you ought to be doing, and doing enough of it. You know why you must do what you have to do about knowing and fulfilling that purpose? The call of purpose never ends. It has no regards for time. It is implanted in our subconscious; it is there in our conscience to remind us, no matter how late the nights of our lives.

The first question of purpose: Are you doing what you ought to be doing? If everyone knew the answer to this question, I doubt we'll need neither this book nor any other on the subject of purpose. If you knew the exact answer to this question, you will not set out in search of your purpose. And oh! How I just wish that by swerving my hand over this book right now, I could spill the answer right into your mind. I'd actually need some lessons in magic to do that.

Research shows that besides the bible, and a few classical timeless books, one of the highest sold books in history with well over 35 million copies sold is *The Purpose Driven Life* written by Rick Warren in 2002. The reason is not so much as in the writer's dexterity (not to take anything away from his grace), as it is in the need people have to understand their mission in life. There are seas of people at sea over what they are here for.

People want to show up before you, and hear you tell them: "This is what you should be doing with your life." Prophecy's a great tool, but it also puts the onus on us to cooperate with God's spirit in fulfilling it.

Purpose discovery is a process, and not an event. The day you hear via prophecy, dream, vision, etc, that this or that is what you ought to do with your life, that day the journey towards full discovery commences. You'll soon find that there are array of alphabets between the 'b' and 'y'. But once you get committed to it, God makes it easier for you to discover. It is truly a hidden treasure.

There is more to life.

A lot of times, it is laughable how people think life ends at this surface. They reduce life to all they can see, taste, hear, smell, feel or live. If anything transcends the food they eat, the clothes they wear, houses they live in, cars they drive, jobs they have, people they date, connections they have with powerful people, family they build, friends they keep and so on, they do not know anything about such, and do not even think it is necessary to know. But they are mistaken because what even gives birth to all that they see, taste, hear, smell, feel or live is in itself transcendental.

Life is first spiritual before it is physical. Do not limit life to the physical, there is much more to everyone than meets the eye. Same way you must dig beyond your physicality to unravel your true mission here on earth, you must spend quality time with your true self to understand yourself. And I am not talking some one hour stuff, I mean it could take you weeks, months or even years to fully come to realizing yourself, but you will also find that whatever time you spent in the search is well worth it.

To make the process shorter and cut the time involved in the search, some people resort to metaphysical means and conjuration of demi- gods. They engage and invoke meta-humanistic propensities to have a peep into the purpose that they are about. They patronize fortune tellers to tell them what the fortune tellers also wish they knew. But I invite you to try the God of all gods, the Creator extraordinaire, the all-knowing Knower, the Architect of destinies before whom all intents and purposes are as clear as the noonday sun. I invite you to come to Him who Himself beckons you to come without pay, come for freely He gives, and you know what? Freely you shall receive and you shall find rest for your soul.

Oh, and how many stories have you heard perhaps of people in their dying days who wished they discovered and lived their true selves much earlier. For anyone who did not do what they ought to have done with their lives, tone of regret is never far from their lips at death should they have the privilege of regret. Somehow it becomes clearer as one age to know what to have done, but it also becomes late to be able to start, so a lot of people just retreat from the initiative. They'll rather live with the regret, and I think that is worse. If all you have is three months of happiness before you bid farewell, as far as you still have the opportunity, maximize it.

An older minister once said to a younger one, "God called you in the morning, you answered Him in the morning, but God called me in the morning, and I answered Him at night. That is the difference between what we will each achieve. I am not the best He has for the now, but I'm grateful that He still gave me a chance." And God is still in the business of giving us all, no matter how old we become second chances at life – to become what He has created us to be. And yes, you can still fulfill purpose in life even as an old person.

2

Life's Three Most Important Questions

WHO AM I?

Have you asked yourself that question before, or you've heard someone answering that question before? It's hilarious what you hear sometimes. People define themselves by their name, their family background, some take it further by describing the school they graduated from (especially if they attended a revered school), their place of work, marital status, and all that. You are probably wondering, so what should it be if not these? Quite frankly, I wonder if there are any more questions to which people find such answers. You know such definitive questions to which only descriptive answers are supplied. Tough question. Who are you?

Not knowing who one is, is the clear reason for some of the poorly-informed decisions and actions that we see in our world today. One who does not know who he or she is, will depend on the definition that others have of him or her, and on that, base his or her life. People who don't know themselves are tossed around by the wave of confusion and misapplication of life. It is such a deliverance to discover oneself.

How do you explain a young man who devotes his life to doing drugs ruining a rather beautiful destiny, saying that someone asked him to do it? He does not know himself. What about a beautiful young lady who for the temporary euphoria, and quick cash that comes with it, leaves home, sleeps with every man that comes her way? She neither knows who she is nor does she value the temple she has. Why would anyone kill themselves and destroy the lives of other people in insurgent and terror attacks? If you ask them, could they even possibly explain why they are doing that? The list goes on and on.

The quest for self-discovery is fundamental to living a fulfilled life. The answer to the question "Who am I?" is in answering another question - "Who am I created to be?" Because we are products of Someone – God and we are created to be somebody.

On the field of play as a kid, my dad called me out. I'd thought he wanted me to go get him something, so it was no-brainer; I just left the pitch knowing that I would soon return to continue my beloved soccer game. And guess what happened? My dad had me sit down, only to tell me I could no longer play the game. And the spirit of protest came all over me. "Why can't I? But my friends are playing. We are not even rough. We are not hurting anybody…" It was an endless lexicon of query. My dad just looked on, let me rant, and whispered, "You are not them, you are not going to be playing soccer in life, why should you spend so much time on it now?"

I know the average kid of this age, already has a position in mind: I could never take that, is it not just to play? blab blab blab… But I assure you, you'll be lucky to have him for a father. And that's not showing off. It is the reality. His unusual depth and wisdom saved me time in life.

I never would have gone far following my soccer hobby. It's not just who I am. I was never created to be a footballer. Of course, I could do some of the stunts kids learn to do, but could that have been my life? I doubt pretty much. I could never leave what I do today for football. Maybe the passion was taken away from me as a kid, but if soccer is my life's purpose, there is just no way it'll go away from me like it has. Don't get me wrong, I still watch good football matches, especially when my country Nigeria plays (with all the disappointments that may come with it), I still enjoy the game, but it has never taken the place of other businesses that I consider purpose-related in my life. It never will. It may be football for me, but something else for you.

Beating Your Mind into Shape

Sometimes you know how that your heart is leading you right but your mind gets in the way. You know who you are, who and what you are created to be, but you just don't want to get down to it. You want to do something else instead of that one, and there could be myriad of reasons for this: You are comparing yourself to someone else, you don't want to be seen as doing that kind of thing, you figured out it's not so lucrative, won't generate money enough for your need, people will laugh at you, that's not the vogue, and the list goes on.

All interpretations that are after-thought given to one's identity, are just what they are – after-thoughts. That you naturally have flair for, get attracted to, and prefer to do certain things rather than others is not your making. Not in all cases. It is the way you have been created. Hitherto, you have been fighting that sweet desire that is welling up on the inside of you, you are letting your mind (your reason) get in the way of your life's mission. You need to watch it.

Sometimes, it doesn't just come the way I have tried to describe above, but you always will find that you have the intra-personal conflict that keeps pulling you in different directions. One is your heart the other is your mind. The challenge is, you can't tell which of the pull is from your heart, and which is from your mind. I admit, that could be a tough job.

God makes it easy for us sometimes when there are people who watch over our lives. People who can see far into the future sitting down than we could ever see climbing the top of a tree. People like my dad who are not only mentors but have spiritual insight and advantage, who, by dint of that wisdom, save us time in life. The time that would have been spent doing something meaningless can now be channeled into pursuing main life purpose. By the way, I still played some soccer as an adult, as a pastime.

Some other times it is God Himself who just causes us, by His incidences to enter into the right places, at the right time, meet the right people, read the right books, attend the right seminars, attend the right churches, get mentored by the right people, dream the right dream, nurse the right vision, draft the right goal or whatever that just order us into our mission in life. I think it gives God as much joy as it does us, that we are able to find our purpose and find it on time, so He plays His part by orchestrating events that line up to bring us that fulfillment.

If He directs your steps, it is your heart that will receive the inkling, the signal, the intuition or whatever you want to call it from Him. He speaks to our hearts. The wisest man that ever lived said, *guide your heart with all diligence, for out of it are the issues of life.* Your heart is the receptor of His calling. Your mind, however, is the reasoning faculty. Your mind processes what your heart has got, and wants to find what's good or bad about it. It also compares that which is in you with that which is outside of you. It is with the mind that you know "this thing is not fitting for my status". It is your mind that gives you all the reasons why you may, or may not do something. And because the mind is filled with all these reasoning, it is louder than the heart.

The voice of the heart is a gentle voice, but firm. In all of the loudness of the mind, you still find that your heart, once in a while, reminds you of something you are refusing to consider, and at such times you either wave it off, or it wearies you to know that you are not doing what you ought to do. The thought of it might not be impressive because your mind is dominating at the moment, but once you get into it, the joy that comes with doing what you should be doing just floods your heart, a drop per time. Your duty? Beat your mind into agreeing with your heart. It takes discipline, and it is possible.

I would not claim that I got to know who I was created to be in black and white from my dad, I really wished he knew it enough to tell me so I could just have a stress-less life, but there were God-incidences that ordered my step into my mission.

The people I met along life's journey both far and near, the books I read, and the passion I discovered was growing in me early in my life. I sat under and listened to a man whose knowledge of the Word and strategy of delivery I doubt there is any who compare directly with, and another whose passion is contagious. I met a man in one night, and found he is in a class all by himself like I desire to be, I read books and other materials by authors whose works were a description of my world, and read volumes upon volumes of biographies of all the great people whose materials I found. I read an average of six books every other month and poured my life into them. As a student in the university, I read more Financial Standard and BusinessDay newspapers than I read books for my exams in school. It was a natural attraction. When colleagues in school came around to read the dailies, I was more interested in business, entrepreneurship, business personality, strategies, finance, personal development, capacity building, etc, and gave myself wholly to those things. Suffice to add that some of my colleagues already could tell that I wasn't normal, and so they avoided staying too long around because we don't speak the same language much. You know what I mean?

What Self-Discovery does to You

Knowing your identity does something to you, as it does to those around you. It opens your eye to know instinctively those you could or couldn't stay around. And people around also know whether they can continue to be around you or their days are numbered. There is just that natural separation that takes place. It's nothing really except that, it delineates the path. Thomas Jefferson once puts it this way: "Do you want to know who you are? Don't ask, act! Action will delineate and define you." People just know their place in your life when you are able to show that you have discovered yourself.

Further, discovery attracts into your life, the people that are most needed on the journey to your fulfillment. It's a magnet, a very effective one at that. The right people that are needed on the highway to your success will be attracted by the progress you are making, they will be impacted by your efforts and will be drawn to you. It's almost automatic. Of course, like magnet, it will also attract those who'll come to perch. They are seeing what you are doing, and they know you are going somewhere so they want to attach themselves to you so you can arrive together. Some are not necessarily a plus to your life; they are just advantage-takers. And there are those who'll think you have to be responsible for them. They come to dump their burdens on you. They'll want to make you feel uncaring and unsupportive when they come to you and you are unable to help them. They never take time to find out if you even have the capacity to help them at the time they came. Such people think because they found some money with you, then they should have some of it. They come around and just take things from your house without your permission and think they just have the right to do that. They may hide under the guise of being brothers, sisters, cousins, in-laws or whatever relationship. Some even come around, and blatantly refuse to abide by the principles on which you have founded your home, and just expect you to fund their trip when they come around without pre-informing you of their coming.

Sometimes, you'll learn to tolerate some of these rude and untoward behavior especially when they come from people you respect, but the time comes when everyone must stand for what they believe and draw the line. Not everyone will go along with you. It is a blessing that you have the courage to let go those who need to go, and drive along with those who need to come along with you. You really ought to be willing, like T.D. Jakes puts it, to let people walk out of your life who want to walk.

You cannot please everybody. Trying to do so is below laudable. It leaves you with displeasing yourself and sure leaves a sour taste in your life. As a matter of fact, no one has the capacity to please everybody. No one. As a philosopher once described it, only a fool tries to please everybody! That some people leave your life is a blessing. It may not so appear at the instance, but as you journey through life, you will find that their leaving opened the door for other people that really matter to come in. It was a blessing that they left.

This is not to say that everyone who does not agree with your position on things needs to go, lest you chase your helpers out of your life. There are foundational matters on which stance must be taken, and there are tag-along matters on which stance can be shifted. If you find that you are not on the same page with someone, you must explore all options to settle the scores, and clear the rift. The person who does not agree with you today might become your closest ally tomorrow. As a matter of fact, true friends must disagree once in a while, and like someone puts it, if two people always agree on things, one of them is either a hypocrite or is not thinking. Conflicts can be resolved, and efforts, frantic efforts must be made to resolve them as they come along.

If you are at a point in your life right now where you are struggling too hard to make a relationship work, be it friendship or business, you need to check it again. Maybe you shouldn't even be in that relationship, maybe there's a better option you are refraining from considering; maybe you are not doing the necessary things to make that relationship work. Whatever the case is, you must step aside from yourself, and if need be, invite the counsel of other people. Check to be sure you are doing the correct thing, and you have done all there is to do. The problem might not be you, it might be them. But you must check yourself first to be sure.

For any relationship to work, both parties need to bring something to the table. Commitment it is called. If you are committed to each other, issues will not linger for too long before they are resolved, communication will not be treated as unimportant. To make the relationship work will be the concern of both parties, but, if you are the one who is carrying the burden for the sustenance of the relationship, it does appear that you do need the relationship more than the other party. And if that be the case, you may need to bear more for the relationship to work. Where both parties stand to benefit, both parties must contribute. On the journey to discovering and fulfilling your purpose in life, whoever and whatever you are killing yourself to take along with you, you must make sure they are even necessary and that they make meaningful contribution to that destiny.

Back to the Source

I did say earlier that, in answering the questions: Who am I? We must ask the question: Who am I created to be? That is because we are creatures of Someone and no one defines a product better than the one who made it.

In making us, there was something in the heart of the Creator, which for all intents and purposes, He wants to achieve through us. Some people He created that they might write to His glory, some to sing, some to dance, some to raise other lives, some to preach the good news, some to fund the preaching of the good news, some to answer to the poverty problems under their sphere of influence, some to eradicate ignorance by imparting knowledge unto others, some to salvage situations, some to create designs and make products that will make others glorify God, some to simply raise a family that God has another special plan for, and the list continues. Great as some of these sound and others not so great, we are not at liberty to choose which we will or will not spend our lives doing! Our lives' purposes are not ours to determine, they are ours to discover!

Don't get me wrong, there are basic good things that every human must give themselves to doing, like caring for others, showing love and compassion to those in need, feeding the hungry, clothing the naked, and sheltering the homeless, even though that might be some people's life's purpose, it still behooves us all to do good unto all men. But there are primary callings, purposes, and life's mission to which every single person has been called, and that is beyond been good to all men. It is more about been good to yourself. You could live the rest of your life making other people's life meaningful while yours is left unattended. How much happiness will it bring you, when you lay upon your bed, and find that you are indeed hiding from yourself by running other people's errands?

When you argue with people about not doing something you ought to be doing with your own life, and instead insist that many people are being blessed by what you are doing, you know in your heart of hearts that, it's not really about the number of people benefitting from what you are doing, it is in most cases, a struggle for you. You are struggling with yourself to accept to do that thing you know you ought to do, and in arguing it loud with others, you are rather hoping to convince yourself and not your co-debaters that what you are doing is what you prefer.

There is no way you are just setting out, launching out into purpose fulfillment, without first finding out, "Who am I created to be?" The One who made you had a picture in mind for you to become. You can never truly know who you are without recourse to the Creator. In chapter seven of this book, there are tests that will enhance the answers to the search, and chapter eight is intended to help you find the true person you are. Suffice to state that, the Creator attached a manual to our lives – a mirror which if we look into, shows a clear reflection of our identity.

The name you bear, the background you have, the schools you attended and the places you work all add up, but they are not your main identity. There is a You besides, and without all of that. So, if you take away all those things by which you currently define yourself, who is left? Maybe that just points to who you are. You are your purpose.

WHY AM I HERE?

Yea sure you are in school right now, at work, with the family at home, in church, on a trip, waiting for someone, etc, but that's not the "here" I am talking about. I am talking about here on earth.

The question above is the second most important that we must answer in life, I believe. Once we have identified ourselves, we must also define our presence. Else, there is no reason for being here. And God did not create someone or something for whom or which He had no intention.

Sometimes when I look at some of the things God made, I really do think that God, men! You got so much time on Your hands to have created this kind of thing. I mean who needs flies, anyway? That have to be swatted when they will not just stop announcing their irritating presence to us? And then, you get to see bats which are primarily responsible for the Ebola virus that has notoriously killed thousands in Liberia and Sierra-Leone alone, and would have done same if not properly curtailed in other parts of Africa, Europe, and America. I mean who need bats, though? I really got curious about why God would waste time making worms, mosquitoes, and all these kind of stuff. Why did God make sure these annoying things got out of His production line?

In my search I discovered something.

I discovered that the activities of flies help to produce a richer soil. The Sphaeroceridae for instance feeds on decaying food or carcasses and thus quicken the cycling of the nutrients and enrich the soil.

Flies are active flower pollinators. The same job that bees do. They eat nectar, lay eggs on flowers and pick pollen with their feet.

If you like birds and fishes, you ought to consider letting flies live because young ducks and shorebirds feed on flies and other insects for survival. Because of their ability to live in salt lakes where most insects can't, flies constitute a major food material to fishes and birds in those regions.

Flies control pests. In fact, it is discovered that some farmers introduce several species of flies into their farms instead of using pesticides only because flies have rich meal in some of those insects that could be considered pests.

Flies are known to contribute to controlling eutrophication. They help to stop the spread of algae over aquatic life, in essence giving life to the water body.

Bats and frogs, in addition to fishes and birds mentioned earlier also feed on flies.

On onegreenplanet.org, in an article titled: *Why Bees are Important to Our Planet*, by Jessica Tucker, it read in a line "Our lives – and the world as a whole – would be a much different place if bees didn't exist" and I thought, yea, sure, it would be a much better place without those stinging irritants. Until I read the next few sentences which stated: "To illustrate this fact, consider these numbers: bees are responsible for pollinating about one-sixth of the flowering plant species worldwide and approximately 400 different agricultural types of plant." For clarity, the same article defined pollination as: "the transfer of pollen from the male part of the flower, the anther, to the stigma, which is the female part of the flower. Upon the two's meeting, a plant's seed, nut, or fruit is then formed." John Haltiwanger on www. elitedaily.com added that, "To put this into context, these are many of the crops pollinated by bees: Almonds, apples, apricots, avocados, blueberries, cantaloupes, cashews, coffee, cranberries, cucumbers, eggplants, grapes, kiwis, mangoes, okra, peaches, pears, peppers, strawberries, tangerines, walnuts and watermelons. Without bees, these crops would cease to exist." God forbid. Please God, increase the number of bees in this world. We just can't do without some of those fruits. And more saddening he added, "Yet, the simple fact is, if bees didn't exist, neither would humans." With what he said earlier, I couldn't agree more.

Rachel Balik in 5 Animals We Need to Survive, available at findingdulcinea. com shared this: "Every scary-seeming vampire bat has a purpose. Their saliva may be an essential factor in developing a blood-thinning medication that could help treat stroke victims" She added that "…food and waste are placed in the bin and decomposed by the red worms. Worms can, therefore, cut down on waste accumulation and provide useful fertilizer at the same time."

Uhm… you'd say. If the submissions above are anything to go by, quite frankly, most of these things constitute stuff we can't live with, yet can't live without. There is a purpose for which those creatures are here.

The purpose of making a car is to enhance movement – to give motion. The purpose of television is to add visuals to otherwise audio only. The purpose of clothes is to cover nakedness. The purpose of food is to silence hunger. The purpose of water is to quench thirst and make clean. The purpose of…, everything has a purpose for its creation. Everything. Everyone.

There is a Natural Grace for it

Naturally, we wouldn't really struggle so badly to live out the true purpose for which we are created and for which we are here on earth. Although it could become challenging sometimes. I mean, life could just come up lemons many a time, but, if we are living out the true purpose for our creation, there is a natural (supernatural, if you like) grace to carry through with our assignment. Whether that purpose brings us fame, wealth, glory or not, it will be that we just enjoyed our lives; we just had fun doing what we should be doing and all these things just came along as accompaniments.

If we discover our purpose, people will pay us to live it. A soccer player on the field just plays, and people pay him to play. A musician just plays, and people pay him to play. A poet or writer just plays (with words), and people pay him to play with it. You will find fun doing what you are created to do, no matter what that thing is, and people will pay you to play. You might want to argue that some jobs are not to be so taken lightly, they require maximum seriousness. Actually, all jobs do. If the person doing it is created to do that job, no matter how serious it is, he will enjoy it so much that, what appears to others as "serious" is "just another day at doing what I love to do" to him. You know why? There is a natural grace that attends the performance of purpose and makes the "serious" work play.

There is enormous attention to details doctors requires when examining someone's body or cutting through someone in a surgical procedure. I doff my hat for that. I was not around when that kind of patient attention was being distributed. The Creator had finished creating my batch when He started with doctors. The patience that counselors sometimes have when helping some people out of troubles that they may have brought upon themselves in life, I bet you, the spirit of slap just comes all over me. Drivers can be at the wheel for several hours in a day just enjoying the art or science of whatever they do. How boring that is to me. Yet, when some of my friends who are in these professions come around to my meetings and they hear me talk, or come to my writing desk, and see me surrounded by this library of books or doing some writing, they really confess how that is beyond them to do. One did confess that, he'll freeze to death standing in front of an audience to give a speech.

We are all graced differently, and must discover our areas of grace, and live it out.

We Are Created To Create

If you ever read the creation story in the bible, Genesis One, the twenty-sixth verse looks somewhat of the passing of the baton to my mind. You see something like: "Let us...let them..." That looks like someone is saying, we have done our part, and they've got to do theirs too. The bulk is passed down. Someone is going to have to take it further from where another stopped. You know when we give birth to children, in those children are leaders. When we become old as parents, we expect that the leadership baton is automatically picked up by our children, especially the first among them. That is why it is oft-unrealized what pains parents go through when their children don't wake up to responsibilities in life as expected of them.

The Creator created us to perpetuate the work He finished. The task of creation is continuous. It evolves. God knew that someday these people that He has created will need food to eat, so what did He do? He gave us plants and animals. It is left to the creative wisdom of man, to process the plants into edible forms, and to kill and cook the animals so he can eat. Right now, man has even stepped it up, he knows how to preserve these materials given by God in cans until months or years later when it is shipped elsewhere or he is ready to eat them. The Creator knew that man will need to live in a shelter, so He gave us stones. The creative wisdom of man converted the stone to walls within which he lives. The creator gave us trees, and in the trees lie our furniture and upholstery, the roof over our heads, and even the book you are holding in your hands right now. We were given plants, and in them are hidden the clothes that we wear. We were given animals, and they wear our shoes around in their skins. We have natural resources, and in them lay the wealth of nations. The soil we step on every day contains everything we will ever need as far as we are here on earth. Those who learn to convert it, further the creation purpose. You are created to create. You are created to further the works of God. It is in doing this that we bring Him glory. I think God just gets all smiles when He sees someone has discovered what else to do with what he has already given, and He says in his heart, "that's why I sent you down there."

Doing Something Until…

Getting to hit the ground running with this whole could really be a lifetime job, but while you are at it, there is something you could get busy doing. While you are trying to figure out what brought you here, you could get yourself doing something until…

We all just need to occupy.

If you set out looking for the job that fits into your identified purpose, and it's taking time to find; if you set out trying to set-up a business, program or mission that fits the description of your calling, it may really take a while before you find it like you may have noticed already. In the meantime of your search, you need to get your hands dirty. No, I am not talking about doing stuff you are not proud of. You need to get your hands busy with work – whatever keeps you going until you get what you desire. If you just want to wait until the perfect job comes for you, my friend the end to that wait might not be in sight. But you can still learn a lot, keep life going, and ultimately prepare for your purpose manifestation. I'll give you an example. If you discover your purpose is about raising children and imparting healthy values in them for a fruitful living, you probably need to be thinking of starting a school of your own where you can structure the training programs to accommodate this calling of yours. Starting a school requires money which you may not have at the moment, so, the way to go is, get into the teaching profession, and find ways of introducing some of your knowledge in this area. You could even liaise with the school owner on this. You get to learn the challenges you are going to face eventually, the better ways to implement your program, you will be better exposed, and so on. That is definitely better than waiting until you are able to gather enough money to start your own school.

Let me tie this all up here. The moment you can answer the question: who am I? You unlock the answer to the question: Why am I here? So, again, dig deeper into yourself, and unravel the mystery that you really are.

WHERE AM I GOING?

"If a man does not know where he is going, everywhere looks like it."

Purpose is both a process and a destination. No one sets out to fulfill purpose and does not arrive somewhere doing so. Purpose fulfillment is fulfillment in life. If you get busy in the room of life pursuing your goals, fulfilling your purpose, having fun with your work and loving God, if you hear a knock, success is who you find at the door.

When we start anything, we sometimes have an idea where that thing leads us. Sometimes things just get out of hand – I mean, you never knew it was going to be this big, but as you got along with it, it kept enlarging, maybe, even beyond your capacity to handle. We expect our endeavors to work out real great, sometimes they do, sometimes they don't. That expectation that we have, in a way, forms the destination of that endeavor. So it is with our lives. We really do ask ourselves sincere questions when all the attention is down, when all the paparazzi is gone, when it's time for bed, and one of those questions is: Where am I going?

Where am I going with my life? Where am I going with these things that I'm doing? Where am I going with this kind of attitude? Where is this effort, activity or job taking me? Is there a sweet ending to this endeavor? Is there an end worth chasing after with this activity I'm engaged in? These are some of the questions that are so locked up in our hearts that our spouses on the same bed with us really don't know we are nursing.

It is the fear of new families whether they can weather the storm that arises in marital relationships especially considering the high rate of marriage failures today. It is the fear of new parents whether they can parent the children they are having the best way possible that make those children compete perfectly with their peers in life and not veer off the path they want them to tread. It is the fear of newly employed whether they will be able to please their employers enough to maintain them on the job especially if they are started on probation. It is the fear of every new leader whether the followers will trust them enough to steer the course of the group. The end is always in sight. We are always asking the question. At least most people do.

I once read that James and John saw people climbing a mountain in haste, and they decided to join. Someone met them along the way and asked, "Hello James, hello John, where are you guys going?" "We don't know, we just saw everyone climbing and we decided to follow" they replied. While most people spend endless time unraveling their destination in life, it is sad that some people just follow. They live life as it comes. They do what every other person does, and just hope that everything will be okay. No, it will not.

Life is by design, someone said, purpose is the design. There is no accidental life. Even accidents are caused. What you find today, is caused by something or someone yesterday. T.D. Jakes roared in one of his life-changing messages: Nothing Just Happens! If you find anyone succeeding overnight, I assure you, he had a long night. There is cause and effect factor in all of life. There is a destination to aspire to, a place to arrive at when all is said and done. But if you are going nowhere, I promise you, you will get there.

If we know that we are heading somewhere, why don't we just head towards that place? If we have the faintest idea that there is an end to which every effort of ours will lead, why do we spend most of our time off-track? Most people are not true to themselves in life. They avoid looking at the mirror of life. They do not even want to look at the reflection of their own faces except to make up. Most people can't stand what they see when they look in the mirror, not for any medical condition, but for the dread of where what they see leads.

I find it amusing the cosmetic lives that a lot of people live. When they are in the public glare, they are so glamorous, so takeaway you could make moral mistakes. They do everything they can to make you see what they want you to see. They drive down an image in your mind and hope that it remains so. That is so cosmetic. This is the kind of life the younger ones want to live because they swallow the pie that they are sold. The paparazzi, the razzmatazz, the *swag* and *effizy* (in Nigerian terms) are everything but real. Most of these people who paint these lives outside, suffer so much inside them. They feel so empty, some of them so used, some so fake, and some just get to help suppress their emptiness with drugs. Little wonder, the world has lost count of celebrities whose lives ended in not-so-desirable conditions. Just be real to yourself. Realize that whatever you do or don't do will take you to an end.

Sometimes when we don't do what we ought to do, it is not just about trying to please our desires, or that we are lazy or that we feel those things will not bring us happiness. No. Most times it is rather that we feel we do not live up to other's expectation of us. We have an idea of how people view us and are so conscious of their perception that it has become a determinant of what we do with our lives. We have given others the power to make us happy or not.

What a shame! No one should hold the key to our lives in that manner or in any fashion at all. As children or growing people, we need the guidance and tutelage of parents and older ones. As we grow older, however, our discovery comes alive in us and beckons us for fulfillment. When that time comes, we know it. And when it comes, we must wake up to its beckoning. We cannot allow other people who don't even know anything about our lives nor have contributed anything to it, to determine the end we must strive for.

And talking about end still, life itself has an end. When the curtain of life is drawn, what end stares at you in the face? Mathew Ashimolowo once quoted, "death to some is an end, to some, it's an enigma, to us it's an entrance." In case you think when life is gone from us, then that is all, you lie. There is life after death. I do not mean to scare you, but since I'm talking about the end, then I might as well tell you that, all of life, even knowing one's purpose is meaningless if there is no thought and preparation for what happens after life. We could either have life after this life or have eternal damnation after it, it all depends – on who we accept and believe in or not. There is only one way to life after this life – Jesus is that way. You might obliterate this part from the book in your hand, it changes nothing. Maybe you don't even like the name Jesus, it doesn't change the fact that you need Him. Actually, you have been missing a whole lot not being with Him. He beckons you today do not harden your heart.

3

Purpose Bewilderment

I'd been engrossed in the writing of one of my books, and it gets so bad some times that I'd forget I've not had my meal. In the middle of the writing, I remembered that I needed to pick something from a room in the house, but as I entered the room, you couldn't help but laugh at my puzzled look. I was startled. Why did I come into this room? What did I need? What brought me here? I forgot what I came into the room for. I was bewildered. I paced up and down the room hoping to pick up the answer to my puzzle in my pacing. It wasn't as much about me forgetting why I came into the room as it was about me asking me whether I was so old I couldn't remember the purpose for which I stood up from my writing desk. I don't even know if it really has anything to do with old age.

I cannot possibly tell you what happened but my mind played a fast one on me. How it did I cannot tell, but does that happen to you too? I guess it does. Do you also forget reasons why you entered into your room? Do you call someone and are trying to remember why you called and have to call back when you eventually remember? Do you make strenuous efforts to remember what you have been thinking about? Does your mind play a fast one on you too? Do you know how painful it could be when you can't figure it out? And you know that happens in split seconds when something just steals your attention, and that's just enough to make you forget what you are really about.

In life, we sometimes enter into rooms of distractions, relationships, difficulties, pressures or even life-threatening situations that make us forget our purposes, and except you don't live in this world, you will have to deal with distraction.

COPING WITH DISTRACTIONS WHILE FULFILLING PURPOSE

This could readily pass as a topic for discussion with youths but it really doesn't end with them.

A man drives along the highway and notices a scantily-dressed lady, while he's going forward on the wheel; his eyes never leave the rear mirror. As he struggles between focusing on the wheel and the lady, he runs into someone else's car on the road. Distraction. While you really think you got something to do in the office, then someone – a colleague perhaps, comes along with a very interesting gist, and before you really gave thought to what you are doing, two hours have passed by, and you are left with no choice but to hurry up to complete the task for which that time was originally allotted. Distraction. The agenda for the meeting is set, and just as you set about achieving the purpose for your gathering, a member digresses with "I think we should..." or "I remember..." and the discussion takes a totally different turn. It's twelve noon, the meeting has to close, purpose not achieved. Distraction. A public speaker becomes engrossed telling an illustration or discussing a current issue of national interest different from his core theme for the program until the time allotted to him expires, then he quickly reels out points he would otherwise have effectively discussed in ten seconds. Distraction. We are in a gathering, with a powerful message going on, and then suddenly we remembered that we should not miss the birthday party of a friend, and off goes our mind wandering which cloth we should wear to the event. Our mind gets us engaged in that until the message is over. We couldn't come up with any particular cloth, didn't get anything from the message. Distraction.

Don't we see these things and experience them? There's something to distract us as much as we like to yield. One of the biggest of them all, probably, since the forbidden fruit in the Garden of Eden is the television.

Actually, screenplay, whether on television, computer, tablet, cell phone or any device at all.

Oh! How destinies are stuck to screens! People really don't consider the non-estimated hours they spend before the screen as anything, hardly do they even think about it. Three, four hours pass and you really didn't know that much time had been spent. The distraction box called the television could keep you busy all your life if you choose to be faithful to it. News run every thirty minutes, movies play twenty-four hours of every day, and there are tens of channels you could tune into depending on the bouquet you subscribe to, and if you really don't like the movie or the show on, you only need to send the remote on an errand. Producers of the television sets keep making it easy every other time, such that there are voice recognition systems on televisions these days that just by saying a word, you could put them on, off, increase or lower volumes, change channels maybe, and that just make you have less use for the remote control and draws you closer to the screen, so you could watch some more with even more ease.

Sadly enough I doubt that producers of the TV sets spend so much time before the set watching it except perhaps to get news that concerns their business, or assess the functional efficiency of their products. Not so the average mind that watches things happen. People create so you can watch, when will you create so others can watch?

The number of hours required to be an expert that could produce a TV set or a show on the TV is so small compared to a lifetime that if not that you have been watching so much; you'll probably have produced your own TV brand or program by now. People get awarded and become renowned for producing great brands or hosting terrific shows on the TV, I've not heard of anyone celebrated for watching so much of the shows, maybe you have.

In Nigeria, the unavailability of a regular power supply is the biggest blessing to some people's lives. Were it not for the inefficiency of the power company - PHCN (or what's their name now anyway), some people would never take their eyes off the TV. But there is no regular power so while the movie is on-going, the power goes off, and because perhaps, there's not enough fuel in the power generator, the movie is suspended until later in the day, and the intervening period is then used to achieve something meaningful for the day.

It's ok to see a movie once in a while, and listen to news when it comes time for it, but you know that's not what I'm dissuading you from. I'm discouraging you from the distraction that has become an addiction for you. If all this book does is to take you away from the television for a while and help you concentrate on something more impactful, then it has achieved its purpose.

Another tool of distraction for this age is the social media. While some use the platforms for meaningful interaction, others just practically live there making no gain whatsoever from the platforms. Today, the social media has literally replaced friendship. Loved ones no longer spend time with each other. It is possible couples are in the room and are completely oblivious of each other's presence. What used to be fellowship among family is now almost completely eroded. Parents talk to kids these days and the kids do not even take their eyes off their devices as they respond to their parents. The social platforms, despite their advantages, have taken sensibilities off a lot of people and have derailed a lot from their main purpose in life, because if only they'll spend half the time they spend on the social media on pursuing their life goals, they'd long have achieved them.

Yet another tool of distraction is games. Games are so rife that they are on every device – TV, phones, computers, other devices created specifically for it, etc. Not only is it a distraction, brain research demonstrates that 8-plus hours of game playing accounts for the atrophy of the prefrontal cortex and parietal cortex of the brain, which controls motivation and concentration. Leonard Sax in *Boys Adrift* (2007) stated that American boys are disengaged because they spend an inordinate amount of time playing video games.

Yet another distraction is friends, so-called friends, most of whom you would do better without. You cannot possibly be friends with everyone. It is not your life's mission to keep friends.

Pause.

To cope with distractions as you set out in achieving your purpose in life, use these simple five steps procedure:

a. Know that there will always be distractions; you are the one who will choose your response to them. If you are looking for something to distract you, I assure you, you will find more than enough.

b. Identify what exactly distracts you. We all respond to different distractions.

c. Choose your response to distractions long before they come. You can make up your mind to carry out a particular assignment, and even in the face of your favorite program on the television, you insist on running through with that task for the day. Missing that program or chat will not deplete you or take anything away from you. You have attached so much fun and excitement to watching that show, so much that when you don't watch it, your brain makes you feel you have been denied that fun. You could make the same of your work. Shift that fun and excitement to your purpose pursuit. It is completing your task that leaves you a better person.

d. Identify your purpose and start working on it. With effective concentration, nothing could get the better of your attention.

e. Concentrate more on what you are doing. Like the popular saying, think about what you are thinking about. Put more of your energy, time and heart into that thing that defines you and you'll find that automatically, you have less and less time for the distraction.

COPING WITH PRESSURE WHILE FULFILLING PURPOSE

Life throws a lot at us, and except you are not really living, you are going to have cause to ask yourself, "Why me?" It could get really bad sometimes. As a matter of fact, every time you are making efforts to get to a greater level in life, there are almost always equivalent pressures waiting to be handled.

If you are doing something worth doing, you are never going to be free from pressure; you will always have to deal with them.

Pressures comes from deadlines on assignments, non-cooperating colleagues at work or business, non-understanding spouses, unstable relationships, unfaithful partners, threat of termination at workplace, inadequate finances, family issues, wayward children, children into drugs or gangs constantly having issues with the law, economic downturn, creditors' pressure, ill-health, spiritual-related issues, etc. although most people's pressure are finance-related, it's different strokes for different folks. Coping with these is something we wake up to do every day, and having to do that in the face of maintaining focus on one's purpose? Quite an ordeal I must admit.

A man, in a story I once heard, was on his way to committing suicide because of the enormity of problems he had. He thought however that he might check with the pastor of an open local church, and at least leave a word with someone so that others can get to know what had happened to him. "Well, I just thought to let someone know in case anyone asks where on earth I am, I am going beyond. I'm on my way to hang myself, and don't even think about discouraging me because it is too late" he started. The pastor looked at him and wished him safe passage to beyond. The man looked startled "wouldn't you even ask why I want to die?" Quite frankly, you'll never really know how unwilling you are to die until you or someone else puts a gun to your head or a knife to your throat. I tell you, in a split second, you'll prefer to live.

Anyway, the pastor looked at him and said: "I know why". The man asked to be told. "You have problems," the pastor said. "Quite on point" the man retorted, "life has been so unfair to me…" the man stuttered along. Then the pastor stopped him, pulled out sheets of paper and asked if the man would be willing to write down these problems. "If it makes any difference" the man replied. Then the pastor pulled out another sheet for himself. Bewildered, the man asked, "What's that for? You got problems too?" "Yes," the pastor replied, "and I thought I might write mine down as well." The man must have thought 'you think you have problems until you have met me.' Anyway, one long silent hour passed by and the man was through writing; the pastor was still writing and had more sheets to fill in another hour. Exhausted and tired of waiting, the man asked that the pastor stopped writing. They exchanged sheets. The pastor was through reading the man's problem list in few minutes while the man spent countless minutes trying to digest each of pastor's problems.

Not only did the pastor have overwhelming problem list, the weight of each of the problems were unequally depressing. The man got up on his feet and headed for the door. No one said a word to each other. The next day, the pastor's phone rang, it was the voice of the man – "if you have so many problems and are still breathing, I was a fool to have wanted to die, and I'm sorry I was."

Pressures sometimes might come from places least expected, people most trusted. People do things that keep the mouth agape in amazement. There is no end to where pressures come from. How do you explain, for instance, a husband's shock when he suddenly discovers that his wife had secretly changed the titles of documents of ownership of their house and other properties? How do you describe a woman's shock who after ten years of marriage suddenly discovers that her beloved husband had actually been married to another person before, and has had children in that union too?

Words have perhaps not been invented yet to describe the pressure some people go through as a result of other people's action; and there are extreme, life-threatening ones that the scope of this book does not and cannot cover. Question is, is it possible to maintain focus on one's purpose even in the face of all these? Answer: a difficult Yes, it is possible. I never said it is easy.

First, you must realize that the pressure that life has brought you are not such but as is common to man. You are not the only one going through. I don't know how comforting enough that sounds, but if you'll check enough, chances are that you'll find someone with a worse experience maybe not very far from you. The knowledge that the problem was not created specifically for you helps to at least appease you.

Second, you must examine to know whether you are on track. You must be able to confirm that what is happening to you is happening because you are doing what is right. Are you doing the things you ought to be doing? Are you doing them well? Challenges come at you sometimes because you are on track going somewhere. Brothers and sisters, people and principalities won't just fold their hands and watch you arrive. You've got to fight; you only have to ensure your fight is worth the effort.

Third, you must keep hope alive that you are surviving and overcoming all of these things. Once hope goes out the window, victory walks out the door. If others overcome, you can overcome too. Wake up every day and remind yourself that 'this too will pass.'

Fourth, you must continue to build in the storm. That's quite a dose there. The only reason you look forward to another day is because of what's in that day. Now if you can't find something in your new day, put it there. Create something you will want to wake up another day for. Put your purpose in front of you, generate so much thirst and hunger for it that you look forward to the next day. Once you become so passionate and obsessed with that vision, it will eventually become your ultimate drive, and erode the pain of your challenges one day at a time. I guarantee you will look around for those challenges, and they are all gone, you won't even know when they were dealt with. You'll simply not find them around anymore. And you know the double advantage? You will also be fulfilling your dreams as you overcome your challenges. Isn't that beautiful?

Fifth, you must continue to pray as you continue to strive. Prayer strengthens. Prayer heals. When you pray, you reach out to the hand that is stretched to help you. It might not come like magic, but you'll find that you are willing to try again, you have more assurance that it will work out well. And the stream of prayer just washes away your heavy pain and helps you heal faster.

Resume.

Sometimes, the pressures we face are not the types described above. We sometimes face peer pressure. With this kind of pressure, we do things because of our social circle. We do things our social group does whether good or bad.

When one faces pressure from the social group, the group's action reflects in that person's action. The person wants to go where the group goes, dress like the group dresses, eat same, drink same, talk same, and do things in a whole lot of ways like them, and other people's lifestyle, action or inaction just redefine that person's life.

On the other hand, as a result of feeling despised, inadequate or neglected by the social group, an affected person can begin to act in certain ways to prove that he or she can survive, create an image or make some kind of statement without the social group. Reactions may be positive or negative depending on the perception and interpretation that person gives to the scenario.

We all face these social pressures whether young or old, only some people have grown in their handling of such issues than others. While some appear unperturbed by the development, some will do anything to join the bandwagon and get in on the fad. The question to consider here is how do we still maintain our focus on our purpose, and not get swayed by this kind of pressure?

First, you must realize that at every level in life, there is a social class that can influence you. So, that you are facing one now does not mean anything different.

Second, you've got to make your choice, and make it early. Who are your friends, who are they going to be? If you don't choose your friends they will choose you. Your friends tell a lot about who you are. Are you ready to be defined by the identities of your social group? Is there a future with these friends? Are you heading in the same direction? If you are, with these people, how soon does it look like you will get there?

Third, after asking yourself these soul-searching questions and you find they are not really your friends, you have to make up your mind to choose the temporary pain of separation for the eternal gain of fulfillment because there is always an end to everything, friendship inclusive. If those friends won't take you to that end, choose to separate from them on purpose. Attach so much pain to being with them. Attach the pain of losing out on fulfillment in life to being with them. Whenever you are with them, see yourself as a loser – on the things that really matter. It won't be long before you don't want to be with them anymore. But if they are your real friends, congrats, consolidate on that relationship.

Fourth, remind yourself of who you really are, and where you are going. You can't be lost among friends. You need to see yourself as one who leads friends into the future, and not otherwise. Of course, it's ok that you learn lessons from people as much as you possibly can, but if your vision means anything to you, it is high time you reminded yourself of that. This is not a one-day, one-stop shop exercise. Do it repeatedly until you are on track to fulfilling your purpose.

THE MID-LIFE CRISIS

Wikipedia submits that mid-life crisis is a term first coined by Elliott Jaques referring to a critical phase in human development during the forties to early sixties, based on the character of change points, or periods of transition. The period is said to vary among individuals and between men and women. Most literature seems to agree with this origin as well as the definition of the concept as given above.

Have you met some people who are obviously dissatisfied with where they are in their lives now, or maybe you are one yourself? It is not uncommon that people take their dissatisfaction out on their family. They blame their wives for pushing them into making decisions that have brought them economic woes. They blame their children for being so insensitive to their economic incapacity. They blame their parents for not leaving them inheritance as other parents do. They blame themselves for being so stupid in the decisions they have made in their lives. There is enough blame to go around, and everyone who is around in their lives gets some of it.

At this stage in their lives, people tend to see how poorly they compare with their contemporaries, and they just can't answer the questions they are asking. It's mostly negative at this time, and although some people just seem to not know what mid-life crisis looks like, others seem to know it too early.

If someone begins to work early enough in their lives as a youth, and they have been responsible for a lot of things around them, people look up to them, and they have been able to have a good life in the days when they started out, the tendency for that youth to think that life is just going to be as good as it always has is very high. When storms come in life, and they will come, it could trigger the mid- life crisis for that person. So you could actually find that in his thirties, that kind of person is already experiencing a crisis situation.

For some inexplicable reasons, some people just go through life, and everything just goes for them as planned. They have all they could possibly ask for, and they go through life like that. Except for the definition of self, there are hardly any questions in their lives that resources are not available to answer to. It is just the way it is for some.

But for most of us, whether you belong in the first category or the second, things are just not going to be the same they have always been.

You hair will not always be so dark, some gray will appear somehow, you may even notice that you are becoming bald. There will be wrinkles on your face as you age; you don't have to have sinned for that to happen. You will not have the strength of a youth when you hit sixty and that's not because someone wants you sick. Like the popular saying goes, forty is the old age of the youth, and fifty is the youth of old age. There will be biological transitions; there will be andropause in the male and menopause in the female. You will become old as far as you are alive; the only way to escape old age is to die. As a woman, your body will not always be in perfect shape like the body of a sweet sixteen, no matter what trimming, suction or whatever medical make-up or surgery you do, that is just the way it is. You will be tempted to put your trousers on your navel as a forty-plus old man. That is just the way it is. Most old people will desire to have things much simpler than they have always had it, and, wait for it… they will not always want to have sex twice a day. Things will change; life will not be the same. You will change too.

Employers will seek far younger people. You will grow dissatisfied with your job. Your savings will not reflect your expectations, and the list goes on and on. I did read up some stuff on Huffington post. They asked some respondents on their Facebook page what the signs are that one is having a mid- life crisis and these are some of the responses as posted on their website:

- When you start panicking about health issues

- When you start to have more questions than answers; especially hard ones: 'Is this all there is?'... 'Why am I doing this?'... 'What about what I need?'... 'Who am I anymore?'... 'What is the real point of me?'... 'Why put my life off any longer?'

- When you start comparing yourself more and more to your more successful friends and younger co-workers and you start feeling increasingly regretful and self-conscious

And the list continues.

People deal with this crisis in many ways. This ranges from trying to pacify and console themselves by buying new things: furniture, cars, beach home, having a new date, etc. to moving out of home or even having a divorce with their spouse.

Change happens. As it stands, it is the only constant.

The first thing you must do in this situation is to accept that things have changed, and change has come to your life. Realize who you have become. As simple as that sounds, it is the inability to want to accept this change that leads people to do things to fight the change. Some medical procedures might not even be necessary were it not for this fight (admittedly some of these might be related to some other reasons). The change in gender procedures, butt enhancement, liposuction, lip work, and all related stuff would not even come up at all.

In all, one thing stands out as the reason for the mid-life crisis: lack of fulfillment. That lack could be a feeling or reality. If people realize that they are not fulfilled, they face the crisis. Accept who you have grown up into, don't fight it. Of course, I do not have a right to tell you what you can or cannot do with your life. I am not telling you to not do something about your bulging tummy or your receding hair. What I am saying is, you can only keep people guessing so far. Whatever you do, the reality is still that, you are who you have grown into, and that growth brings that change you are fighting. When all the make-up is gone, the real person manifests.

Second, you must seek ways to make the most of your current reality. What can you do with what you have? And you might be wondering: What do I have? Age. Age is what you have. Is it an asset? Well, it depends on how you gathered it. If you gathered it well, then it came with experience and by extension, wisdom that is an asset that can be of great use to a lot of people, and help you and others get to the future that looks elusive faster than otherwise. You must find ways, new ways of deploying this experience and wisdom that you have gained to further your lot, and to contribute to making the lives of others less stressful. People can always gain from what you have if you find a way of getting it across to them.

Third, fulfillment is still very possible for you. You can discover your purpose for living, and use the rest time of your life pursuing that purpose. It will be a treasured discovery for you. Set time aside to look inwards, commune with yourself, commune with God, and interact with people you believe can be of benefit to you in your pursuit. I have no doubt that you will find if you seek. And friend, it is worth searching for. In the search is happiness, and in realizing it is fulfillment. Wouldn't you rather live the remaining days of your life fulfilling your purpose?

THE CAREER THING

What eventually becomes our career is informed by many a factor. For ignorance of what they really want to do, a lot of people have ended up doing things that bring them far less joy, and have stayed so long in it, they do not know if they can do any other thing.

Sometimes we start out in one field, but may switch as many as four or more before we are past active working age. We are in search of more money, a better working environment, career advancement, and indeed purpose fulfillment, this leads us to keep trying as many careers as we can possibly find ourselves in. Sometimes we confine the search to similar career path or derivatives of our chosen field. For example, a sports person after going beyond the active playing days may become a coach or technical assistant in similar sports. A businessman may keep trying his hands on different businesses. A school teacher may resign from one school only to resume in another school. At other times, though, we go far wide ways from similar careers. A teacher may resign to become a businessman. A medical doctor may become a musician. A nurse may become a career counselor, and so on. These are, in themselves, search for fulfillment.

People study one course in the tertiary institution, and that's as far as it goes, they never do anything in their work life that relates to what they studied in school for four years or more. I do not know about other climes much but I know we are notorious for this in Nigeria. You can enter into a banking hall, and who do you find as a teller? A graduate of mechanical engineering. You can enter into a sales organization, and who do you find as the head of sales? A graduate of veterinary medicine. You can enter a restaurant, and who do you find as the manager? Yea, you guessed right, a graduate of law. Besides the fact that people must do something to keep body and soul together, and that even though we studied something in school, we can have a passion for something else, lack of proper direction in life, among other factors, is on top of the list.

Wouldn't we get to fulfill purpose faster if we knew it earlier? Wouldn't we become better bankers if we just knew that's what we wanted to do, and studied a related course in the advanced classes? Wouldn't we have more educated sales people if otherwise vet doctors studied sales? Or the otherwise lawyer studied catering or business management? Well, I did talk about the influence of parents in determining what their children eventually study in the advanced schools, so I'll not dwell much on that here, but the task is up to us all – the student in the school who is pursuing a career in life, the adult who is already in the workforce and the parent who is playing background roles in all these. Life can be more interesting, and career paths can be more fun-filled, if people discover who they are created to be earlier, and use their course of study in school to further the pursuit of it. We all cannot be musicians; neither can we all be writers; nor business people; nor pastors, etc. we are created for different purposes, and I think God likes variety so much He created enough to give us all at least one area of interest.

Your career will be more interesting, rewarding and fulfilling if it is in the area of your purpose.

When I mention rewarding I do not necessarily mean monetary, although a good reason to work. If the only reason you are working is for the monetary gain, get your bags ready because you will soon need another job. Our careers must be centered on our purpose; nothing should drive one to work more. It doesn't matter if that job is that of a teacher in a poor neighbourhood school, a security officer, a street sweeper, a volunteer in a remote village, a missionary in an unknown land, an unknown forester, an animal tamer, a social worker, whatever that job is called, that name is a mere appendage of people's supposition, that is not what it represents to you. That job is defined as fulfillment to you.

What career is that for which your heart beats? Do not get carried away by the opulence of another fellow's career, you go ahead and dignify that chosen career of yours; it is you who makes the career, it is not the career that makes you. Dignify it, wash the clothes so dignifiedly, and let people look no more for another clothes washer, cook the food so well and let people search no more for another restaurateur, fix the car so well let people know there is no technician like you in that field, teach those students of yours with all that is in you, pour all of your heart into all of theirs, and let their lives begin to reflect their purpose, sing your songs so well and let history have it that you gave it all you could, dignify your career, whatever it is.

4

Purpose In Talents

UNDERSTANDING TALENTS

I checked out the Latin word for Talents in several dictionaries and found that there is more than one word to define it. The following words came up: talentum, facultas, dos, genius, indoles, ingenium, materies, musa, materies. I thought we might examine the probable meanings/ synonyms of some of those words:

- **talentum:** talent;

- **facultas:** faculty, capacity, ability, abundance, talent, capability, feasibility, mental resources, opportunity, resource;

- **dos:** dowry, talent, endowment, gift, marriage portion, quality;

- **genius:** genius, creative spirit, generative power, demon, entertainer, inclination, talent, vital energy;

- **indoles:** native quality, character, genius, inborn character, talent, younger generation, native ability;

- **ingenium:** ingenuity, genius, ability, wit, acumen, aptitude, brain, capacity, ingenious person, innate quality, invention, talent;

- **materia:** material, talent, abilities, wood, lumber, matter, stuff, substance, talent, theme, timber;

- **musa:** muse, genius, gust, song, talent, taste, wit;

I tell you what, I got bored reading some of those words myself, especially the one that had to do with demon or something, I mean who wants one? That isn't some nature's present one craves.

Actually, when I saw the word "material" it reminded me of something. If anyone was so academically intelligent in my class in my local secondary school then, we called them one or both of "bukuru" or "material" I didn't even know how correct that appellation was until I started reading that genius, talent, and material could mean the same thing. How relieving.

Those words more than drive down the concept of talent and how that it comes by special divine providence.

A talent would be a waste if not intended for something specific. A gift is unappreciated if the receiver does not at least examine it. There would be no need for giving a gift if it won't be used. How would anyone know they have genius if they did nothing inventive or innovative? Would the world even know there is abundance of talent, gift, acumen, vital energy, brain or whatever name it's called if it is not deployed? And everyone is given something by divine providence; everyone is given a gift that they ought to at least check, an ability they ought to at least deploy.

Do you feel untalented? Not good enough? Not comparable to others in any way? In truth, it's just a feeling. There is a provision for you. There is something you are good at; something you, you can do so well to the amazement of most people. This natural ability or skill is right there on the inside of you. It's in you. You have to let it out.

Maybe you are still at sea wondering whether you have any at all. You should ask yourself the following questions: What do you want to do? What do you know you can do with relative ease? What do you seem to do well even without having been trained for? What is your idea? What are your dreams? What are your strengths? What areas of life do you gravitate towards more? What is your most constant interest? What things attract you more than others? What is your passion? What are your potentials? What experiences do you have? What suggestions have you received? etc. though no blanket answer, these questions are leading; they help to land you somewhere, somewhere as close as possible to what defines your talent.

Chapter seven is on the various tests you must examine yourself with as you search for your mission on earth. You should never miss reading that chapter painstakingly. For now, let us concentrate on the subject of talents.

TALENTS: THE SEEDS OF PURPOSE

If only I could stop the car in the middle of the traffic and take out my pen and pad and start writing down the flurry of ideas as they cascaded and permeated my soul. Those kinds of thoughts would normally come when I'm at the desk or my computer or in a solitary place where my mind rests upon my heart as my pen rests upon my pad to manifest the strength of its ink. Those kinds of thoughts come at times in the middle of concatenation when I'd have given my soul up to thoughts that only souls ruminate on; they would only come when I'm asleep but awake enough to know where my writing desk is; but sometimes they despise the solemnity and serenity that the mind revels in when it wants to think, and, they could be heard in the speech of a fellow in a conversation; they could be read in the thoughts of others as they put them out in books, newspapers, blogs or other fora; they could come anyway, anyhow, anytime and anywhere. Their timing is determined by forces beyond us; forces that play on the fields of our minds; forces we may not even understand.

In the words of John Wooden, "Talent is God-given, be humble, fame is man-given, be grateful, conceit is self-given, be careful." You played no part in choosing the talent you found that you have; you played no part in selecting the childhood unusual abilities you manifested for which people called you genius. There was absolutely nothing you did that brought your ingenuity out except that you thought you could do that thing, and you did it. You grew up to continue in the realm of that thing or you found something more interesting to an adult mind. If you continued with that thing, you honed it over time, and probably got better trained at it, and people called you expert. There is nothing perhaps more natural than talent.

There is purpose in talent. Talent is the seed of purpose.

The attraction you have for some things or activities are truly inexplicable. Your only explanation is: "I just like it". If you find explanation for what naturally attracts you, you made it up. If you find explanation for what you can naturally do even without any form of training, you are giving credits to yourself, and that is not right. There is nothing you did to become so talented. Nothing, absolutely nothing! What did you do to have a naturally beautiful voice? What did you do to have a mind so inquisitive searching to know things that others would normally overlook? What did you do to have that spotless adorable face that people call beautiful? What did you do to become so tall or so short? What did you do to beget the natural ability that you have? How come you are a male and not female? What part did you play in the choice of your gender? God found that He could pour out into you a measure of that ability, and He did, without consulting you. It could have been someone else, but He chose you. He gave something to you as He did give something else to some people else.

Every natural ability is given to you. It is a grace. The support auxiliary enhancements, those ones you must learn.

A singer is first naturally talented, then he or she gets trained, and that is the enhancement, to make a better singer. The singer can go further to learn how musical instruments accompany the natural voice, and how to adapt the voice to the flow of the sounds of the instruments or even play the instrument and all that. A writer or fine artist is first naturally talented with a conceptual mind, then he or she gets trained either in a writing or art academy or by relating with other people's works, and that is the enhancement, to make a better writer or fine artist. A public speaker, activist and such person is first naturally talented, then he or she gets trained in either formal or informal places or by doing the activities repeatedly over, and that is the enhancement, to make a better presenter. And on and on it goes.

"I did not start out like this, in fact, if anybody ever told me I could ever do what I'm doing today, I could get a bet with the person." How many times have you heard that said? Sure not everybody starts out in life knowing they could do certain things or even showing tendencies of abilities to do certain things, but, a talent is a calling. Calls may not be heeded immediately, but as life will reveal, they will be heeded. That you did not hear your phone ring when someone called does not mean that the person did not call your line. You will get to know that you were called when you check to see your missed calls or you check your voice mail.

Talent is a calling.

You were called from the very beginning before you were born. You never did hear the call, but that does not negate the fact that He called you. The call becomes loud as life unfolds. Your talent is the voicemail or answering machine. Check to see what He called you to do. It is not impossible to find a shy kid grow up to become a public activist or speaker as an adult. The call had been there, the talent grace had been released, but it only became clear as growth came. Now I'm really short for words on how to paint this image, and I can only hope that you truly understand what you are reading. You have been called, whether you heard that call or not, life will tell.

He gave something else to someone else.

You have been called into what you have been called into; you have been given the grace that you have; that is it for you. Every other person has been given what they have been given. Is it not amazing how we take a liking for different things, and even with strenuous efforts, we still don't just like certain things. I mean, why wouldn't you rather be a human rights activist, or a musician, or a sportsman, or a teacher, or a salvager, or an entrepreneur, or any other person than you currently are? What's more amazing? Why can't a typical business writer write a love story typically? Why can't a Robert Kiyosaki write a J.K. Rowling's *Harry Porter*? Why can't a typical soap opera scriptwriter who writes scripts that air for years write a short movie easily? I mean we have few exceptions here and there of people with overlapping abilities, but a typical grace is given for a typical assignment for which we have been typically called. We are given this grace(s) differently.

That is the more reason it's no use trying so hard to be someone else. You are not them and cannot be them! The best you can be of another person is a copy. Why deny your world your grace while you struggle to be someone else? Of course not all talents are for showbiz. Not all talents require you coming on the stage and getting so famous. Not all talents get all the television ratings and airtime on the radio, but no calling is greater than another in the sight of the Caller. It is the called that will have to magnify his call. We cannot all influence the world at the same level. Not all movies will gross two hundred million dollars at the box office; not all books will sell one million copies; not all singers will *Beyoncé* the world and not all footballers will play for Barcelona, Real Madrid, Manchester United, Bayern Munich, Arsenal, Chelsea and all the other big clubs in the world.

There are big stages, and there are small stages; you must only make sure you are on your own stage. Everyone will influence their world. My world may be larger than your world, or yours may be larger than mine, we may only not abandon our worlds in pursuit of other people's worlds. You have been assigned and called to reach a certain people with your own unique delivery of the same message, and those who must hear you to understand the message will hear you if you do your assignment. One of the churches with the largest congregation in Africa and indeed the whole world is the Redeemed Christian Church of God with churches and members in over 110 countries of the world according to the General Overseer of the church, Pastor E.A. Adeboye. But if the pastor of an unknown church in an unknown location with a membership of about ten people will do his assignment as is required of him, he is fulfilled in the sight of the Caller as is the pastor of the largest congregation in Africa. It is foolhardy to pursue someone else's mission. It's like Robert Browning once quipped, "All service ranks the same with God." Of course you should desire better ways of doing what you are doing and make efforts to learn how to get better results than you are getting; you must bear in mind that you are the one to magnify the call you have received and dignify it, but, you must also know your place in the scheme of creation. You will fulfill much more, knowing what your assignment is. My assignment is not your assignment, neither is yours someone else's.

And so in the middle of this traffic comes an idea that would make all the difference in the book I was working on at the time; an idea that requires still and quiet for me to jot and meditate, but nay it would not come when I had that still and quiet, it would come when I'm in traffic, high traffic, behind the wheel. So I resort to begging this idea. Please don't go, stay with me. I kept warning my mind to make sure it arrests this idea and don't let go until I find a suitable place to park the car and write it down. Thank goodness, finally, I berthed my car, brought out my pad which always had a pen attached to it, pulled out the pen, opened a blank page and guess what I remembered: my plea to the idea - "please don't go, stay with me." That was all I remembered. No please don't laugh, this is not funny. I scratched my head, wandered in my mind, twisted my neck, and even chewed my pen hoping to get a clue to the location of the escaped thoughts. No way, I never got any. Frustrated, I asked my mind, "so why did I have to pull over in the first place, should you not have just told me that you couldn't do your job? I know the idea is there with you, and you wouldn't release it to me" and on and on I went. Well, all the ranting meant nothing, it never came back. My mind had won the game again. It's crazy but it's true. The idea escaped my capture.

And how many songwriters will tell you the same about how they couldn't pin down a song early enough until it left them? How many poets will tell you they couldn't box the lines until they had nothing left of it when they were ready? How many script writers will tell you of a story that started to form in their minds when they were not in a position to write it down? How frustrating an experience to have when you know that could be an award-winning story, maybe? It happens all the time to even the greatest geniuses. Ideas and thoughts elude us all. Sometimes they come back same, sometimes they come back modified, sometimes they come back in another form entirely, and sometimes they never come back. It's true. Ideas elude us all. Ask and you will be told.

All of life is replete with elusive ideas and thoughts of both great and small. Thoughts are elusive, talents rust. A talented person may misplace an idea, but unused talents rust and need to be overhauled. There is a need to pick up, clean up and refine the talent that has been left dormant.

And you are graced. Yes, you. You are talented beyond you know. It's been unused because you never thought you had it, or you thought you are not good enough at it. No one's good enough, we are all striving. Only those whose ideas have been seen are praised, and the praised is afraid that their next idea may not receive as much accolade as the last. You are good enough… to at least start. When you progress, criticisms will come but so will praise too, and before long, you will find that you are afraid that your next work will be as good as your last. And that, my friend, is a good place to be.

So if you are like me whose idea seemed to run away, don't stop. Run after it. Give it the Formula 1 chase it takes. Many a time ideas love that you want them, just like a young lady blushes at the interest of a young man that she notices. By the way, did I tell you that I caught up with that idea? Else you wouldn't have this book in your hand. Sometimes we catch up with them, sometimes we don't, but we only need to continue the chase. In chasing after one thing, you stumble upon another, sometimes a better alternative. So don't stop, keep chasing. Be in hot pursuit of your talents. I know it's rusty, but it is not beyond redemption. Find it, pick it up, and refine it. Get someone who can help you with that. Shy not away from making mistakes, it's the first stair up. Make mistakes, get criticized, make another mistake, get insulted, do it again and again, one or more of many things will happen: people will either get tired of criticizing you, you will learn better ways, they will see you succeed and join your train to success island.

The greatness of every tree is in its seed. The width, height, and strength of every tree is in its seed. Where a seed is planted, whether you see it or not, there is a tree there. Like Andrew Wormack once said, "I don't have to be there when you plant your seed to know what kind of tree you'll have, I only have to be there when the tree is grown." On point! People don't get to see who we are until we manifest.

There is a seed of purpose inside us all. It is called talent. I think that God just kind of answered this question of purpose for us before we ever got to ask. He just deposited in us the definition of our being before we ever got to know ourselves. I reckon that, even if your reality is not exactly the talent you have discovered, you have an undiscovered talent that is your reality.

There is no purpose without a natural, nay, supernatural backing. There is none. There is a direct correlation between what you have been designed to become in life, and what you have been given. There is a correlation between the purpose you are called to in life, and the grace you are allotted. What you could possibly do in life is directly proportional to what you have been naturally endowed for. There is the seed in you of the tree you should become. There is.

We do not have a Creator who forgot to give the tools for the assignments He created us for. We came complete; we only go through life discovering how complete we are.

The airplanes that we fly today, the posh cars we drive, the unimaginable ships we sail, the splendor we have in homes we live in, the beautiful gardens and even the grotesque immoral vanity that characterizes today's world, all things good and bad that we have in this world have always been here, with us, in us. The advent of technology and evolution of the environment made some things clearer but nothing new was added to creation. They all came with us, in us. Man only live in life to discover there is a creation in him he needs to bring out, and that is called an invention. We came complete. The seed has always been there. God made us all good, but the seed of corruption came into those who opened themselves up to it, and thus they convert the good of creation to evil. The seed determines the tree.

What seed is in you? What grace have you been given? What talent do you have? Quite a number of questions to ask in light of this; but you should ask, you must ask because in asking there is answering.

HELP, I'M TOO TALENTED!

I've not met many aspiring youths in this age who don't have a multiplicity of talents. It appears to me that God is just pouring out abundance on this generation and giving us no room for excuses whatsoever.

How often have I heard that statement, "I'm so good at several things, I don't even know which one I should concentrate on." Several youths confront me with related questions in my speaking engagements, and, and what can I do?

You are probably struggling with not knowing what to settle down with of all you have been blessed with. You are like a young man, who is due for a marital relationship and has many female friends who are qualified to live with him for the rest of his life. It can be confusing when the male does not know what he wants, and yet more confusing when he knows what he wants. He may have curried them all along so well, every one of them thought they'd be the one. So being a good friend to everyone eventually turns out to be the worst best thing he ever did.

Are you struggling with multiple talents? First, my friend, it shouldn't even be a struggle, what you have is multiple gifts, and it's no curse to be so blessed. Accept and embrace what you have, savor the abundance. Next, find a use for them. Get your hands dirty with what you have; deploy them, engage them; put them to work, and send them on an errand. You are firing up your creative instincts when you do that. As you continue to engage them, you will have an experience comparable to pulverized wheat being sieved. The finer particles are separated to produce the needed flour. You will find, among your gifts, that there are some of them you are more attracted to, and quite naturally, will use more of. You will, when you have to choose, do certain activities instead of others. You will engage more in activities that have a lot to do with your main grace or interest. More and more use of that particular gift means less and less use of the others, and by nature, a perfection of the one you use more is what you have.

A person that sings, writes, acts, does fine arts, fashion designing, etc. will struggle well with which she should concentrate more on. Applying the model discussed above. She needs to use all these gifts. As she uses them, she will find that she uses more of some of the gifts instead of others. It could be that she enjoys using those ones more or that people enjoy her using them more. As time goes on, the list of most-deployed talents even narrows further. She might find that, after some years, she's more of an actress than she is a fashion designer, singer, fine artist or any other thing for that matter. With time she becomes an expert at acting that she just does those other things for pastime only. She falls in love so much with acting that she has lesser time for any of the other would-have-been talents. The young man knows in his heart of hearts, like they say, which of the ladies he's surrounded with would be the best for his life's journey. Of course, as compared with others on his list, using certain physical criteria, she may not compare favorably, just like others don't compare well with her on the most important grounds on which such decisions are made. His heart chooses that lady over others that his mind suggests. Destiny is made.

Extending the critical issue of multiplicity of talents, there is something I tag the derivative use of talents. I actually did write an entire book on this concept; it is titled: *The Onion-bulb Principle: Getting Everything You Can out of Everything You Have,* a little book you could be through reading in one hour, but would leave you a lifetime impact. Your gifting can be likened to the very many strippable layers of the onion. As you remove one, you find another inside.

The gift you have may be a primary gift of talking. From this gift come the layers of public speaking, teaching, public relations, activism, master of ceremonies, comedian, radio host, television personality, and you name it. You can still apply the model discussed above here, whereupon you find that you are more attracted to being on TV than you are to the radio or being an activist or any of the other derivatives of the primary gift. The advantage with understanding primary gifts in this light is that it helps to narrow down the multiplicity so you can know if what stands as confusion is actually from the same root which is called the primary seed, or otherwise. Narrowing it down just makes a lot of difference to the whole concept and makes the adoption and use of the talent much easier. You should get a copy of the book for a full download on this.

5

The Product God Made

THE AMAZING POWER OF THE BRAIN

There are conceptions and misconceptions about the capacity of the human brain. Most notable among them is the ten percent myth – that the average man has not been able to use more than that much of his brain capacity. This submission has been credited to various people including Albert Einstein, James Williams, and Boris Sidis, the latter two due to their work on William Sidis. They were both psychologists with Harvard. Einstein had used the theory to explain his cosmic towering intellect.

A lot of critics have played down the possibility that man used up only ten percent of his brain. As obtained from an article on www.scientificamerican. com, John Henley, a neurologist at Mayo clinic did, in fact, say that "Evidence would show over a day you use 100 percent of the brain." He went further to explain "Even in sleep, areas such as the frontal cortex, which controls things like higher level thinking and self-awareness, or the somatosensory areas, which help people sense their surroundings, are active. Take the simple act of pouring coffee in the morning: In walking toward the coffee pot, reaching for it, pouring the brew into the mug, even leaving extra room for cream, the occipital and parietal lobes, motor sensory and sensory-motor cortices, basal ganglia, cerebellum and frontal lobes all activate. A lightning storm of neuronal activity occurs almost across the entire brain in the time span of a few seconds."

The same site highlighted a line from the comic Far Side by Gary Larson where a student with a particularly tiny head said to his teacher, "Mr. Osborne, May I be excused? My brain is full." Some people have concluded that it is indeed a myth credited to the self-help, self-development people to say that people use only about ten percent of their brain capacity.

Pushing further on the brain capacity, some experts attempted to compare the brain to the computer system, and this is what Paul Reber, professor of psychology at Northwestern University had to say: "The human brain consists of about one billion neurons. Each neuron forms about 1,000 connections to other neurons, amounting to more than a trillion connections. If each neuron could only help store a single memory, running out of space would be a problem. You might have only a few gigabytes of storage space, similar to the space in an iPod or a USB flash drive. Yet neurons combine so that each one helps with many memories at a time, exponentially increasing the brain's memory storage capacity to something closer to around 2.5 petabytes (or a million gigabytes). For comparison, if your brain worked like a digital video recorder in a television, 2.5 petabytes would be enough to hold three million hours of TV shows. You would have to leave the TV running continuously for more than 300 years to use up all that storage." Quite sincerely, how would you like to confirm that what you have above your neck is that capable?

In a lecture delivered at the University of Colorado, Sir John Eccles declared, "the human brain has infinite potential - so how can you calculate a percentage of infinity." Reading through one of the books of the renowned brain surgeon – Benjamin Carson, I also found that the brain has the capacity to retain an image of someone, or to remember someone even after fifty years of seeing the person.

I don't know what you think of what you have, whether you think you have anything comparable to anything described above or you are probably muttering, "Ola Barnabas, May I be excused, my brain is full." I do not know the size of your head my friend, but you can rest assured that your brain which is just about three percent of your total body's weight by the way is most certainly not full.

This amazing organ that God gave to man is infinite. We could never really understand all about it. Someone once noted that God gave us a brain so we could give Him rest. We would never really leave God alone in that sense, but our brains are massive in capacity.

MAN'S SUPERNATURAL CAPACITY

When man was created and put in a garden popularly called the garden of Eden, it would be hard for man to understand the greatness that was put into him, except that God who created him said that He did create him in His image. I guess that means more than mere words. In His image means created to be like Him. You could tell who the father is when you see the son.

The first expression of man's ability was in Adam's ingenuity in naming all animals and plants. I don't know if you've ever given thought to it, but God must have made so many animals and plants that the rest of man will live the entirety of their lives to discover. I mean, we just keep discovering the different species of different creatures, and to think that one man named all these? And whatever name he called them they are called?! It is just incredible.

If anyone ever doubted that man could do anything, not God. As it would turn out in one of the many stories told in the bible, man had made up his mind to build a tower that would reach up to the heavens where he could make for himself a name lest he be scattered on the face of the earth. Had God not intervened, that tower would probably be standing today or we would at least have relics of it. But in a swift reaction, when God saw the progress being made, He moved to confound the people's language and confirmed their fear of being scattered all over the earth. But this He did not do without leaving us a thought. As quoted from the Amplified Version of Genesis Eleven Six, referring to what the people had achieved, God said: "...and this is only the beginning of what they will do, and now nothing they have imagined they can do will be impossible for them." God said that!

That just leaves what is called 'limits' within the realm of man's imagination. That was only the beginning of what man will do! And if the man can imagine anything, he can do it! Have we not seen man dominate his world since? Are some inventions not truly imaginative? Man has even left off from the earth to conquer space. Many inventions did die uninvented if what iconic Myles Munroe said is anything to go by, that the richest place on earth is the grave, because therein lies potentials unrealized, dreams unfulfilled, inventions not seen.

Is it not rather amazing to know that what we have achieved now is nothing compared to what we have not seen, or may never see? Inventions that our children and children's children, generation yet unborn will come up with? If you doubt that, just dig up pictures of technologies that were once the rave of the moment: the large heavy storage device used by IBM which required several men to load on a truck, and which was just 5megabytes by the way, the cars of the days which compared unfavourably with a locomotive, the ink of the days which required the services of the feather of a fowl, the communication mode of the days which required a ship to sail across border to bring the letter in, the breaking news in some climes which would have happened a year before, etc. don't we look at all of these and wonder how people survived in those days? Isn't it just amazing how far we have come in our age and times? And to think that what we have achieved is still going to be thrashed by the generations that come after us and that they might also wonder how we were able to survive? I believe that scripture is really being fulfilled.

Incidentally, imagination could be both positive and negative, but I am talking about positive imagination here.

IMAGINE IT

One of the people that qualify to talk about imagination, I believe you'll agree with me, is a man called Albert Einstein. It appears he had a lot of use for his. These are some of his sayings on imagination as obtained from goodreads.com:

"Imagination is more important than knowledge. For knowledge is limited to all we now know and understand, while imagination embraces the entire world, and all there ever will be to know and understand."

"I am enough of an artist to draw freely upon my imagination. Imagination is more important than knowledge. Knowledge is limited, imagination encircles the world."

"Logic will get you from A to Z; imagination will get you everywhere."

"Imagination is everything. It is the preview of life's coming attractions."

What a submission!

I know a lot of people who argue with their breath that experience is the greatest. Good as experience is, it is of the past. The future can be a complete departure from it. Gleaning from the past is what the wise do as they approach the future, but as they do that, they know that imagination is the main determinant of the future, not experience. Oscar Wilde declared that "anyone who lives within their means suffers from a lack of imagination." And Mark Twain added, "You can't depend on your eyes when your imagination is out of focus." If all we have is experience without imagination, we cannot deliver the future. Man's supernatural capacity is in his imagination, not in his experience.

You might have the tendency to wonder whether you are one of those whose imagination is herein referred; it might be that you have been thinking and relying more on the experience you do not have rather than lift your eyes to the imagination which you are abundantly blessed with. The mine in you is not mined yet, it will amaze you what is in there. You are not a special breed without imaginations, no you are not. The future you seek direly is in you. Your mind is more than a goldmine. You are a bundle of surprises. Your life is a canvas; splash the colors of your imagination on it. You can be all your dreams. You can discover yourself, and be all you are created to be, but you must imagine. You must imagine for that is the determinant of your rise in life. How far can you see? How high can you go? How much can you achieve? How will you compare with others in your world? It's all in your imagination.

The harm that experience brings on is that of limiting us. Experience when taken as a deterministic variable, tells us what can, or cannot be done; what has or may not be done. You just need to look in the face of all these limiting experiences and scream to yourself: I CAN DO ALL THINGS. I once read the story of a young man who showed up in a mathematics class and solved an equation that had been tagged unsolvable. He and colleagues were served the question in the class by the professor (who obviously knew there was no solution) when the test time was over, and the professor was getting ready to laugh at the fruitless effort of the class, he called for them to submit their scripts. Of course, everyone struggled with the question, and nobody solved it; nobody except the man who did not know that it couldn't be solved. You can picture the shock on the face of the professor.

Accomplished imagination becomes experience.

If all you rely on is experience, brother, you have drawn the line on how far you can go. Experience tells you how far everyone before you has gone and gives you the story of the best of them all. Experience expects you to be just one of the statistics of those who made efforts, at best, to reach the record set. Experience is good, but it comes with its limiting factors, only imagination is infinite. If you think you have seen the best, wait until you meet the man that is imagining.

Is there anything people are telling you couldn't be done? Is there anything that you have not seen anyone do yet? Could it be that you are the one, the first person destined to do it? Could you be the Ben Carson to successfully separate the Siamese twins joined together at the back of their heads? Could you be the Bill Gates to make computer software so important that it makes you the wealthiest man alive? Could you be the Les Brown to come from a background that is so low and yet rise to be the biggest name in motivational speaking? Could you be the John Maxwell to change the face of leadership in the world? Could you be the Mark Zuckerberg to redefine social media? Could you be you?

There are infinite possibilities in you, but it is in your imagination. There is a supernatural capacity in you, but it is in your imagination. Imagination literally sets apart one man from another even though both are in the same profession. You may have discovered who you are created to be, but what makes you distinct from others is your imagination. You have discovered your purpose, but what takes you to the summit of it is your imagination. Kurt Vonnegut warned that "We are what we pretend to be, so we must be careful about what we pretend to be." Have you set a standard for yourself already, a height that you consider the best available, you may need to revisit it, collapse it, and double or even triple that standard. Everyone is rich, superbly rich in the realms of imagination. You can't possibly be so poor you can't afford a dream, someone said. Spend the wealth of your imagination lavishly.

There is no greatness without imagination. Mark Buchanan once quipped that, "Revelation is God's method of disclosure, but imagination is the way we receive it." In imagination is hidden revelation. Who you are, and what you are created to become could really be discovered in what you are imagining. There is no Dubai in the UAE without imagination. I mean for a one-time desert some forty years ago to become the number one destination for tourism in the world, imagination played a part in that development. What kind of life do you desire? To what level do you want to achieve greatness with your purpose? Imagine it.

WIRED FOR GREATNESS

A fish does well in the river. It swims and flies albeit without wings; it shows off in its habitat, and appears to enjoy every bit of it, but, should it envy the bird on the tree because of the height, and try to climb a tree, it will soon find that godliness with contentment is great gain. We all need to respect what we have more. We need to love the fact that we are who we are and not someone else. We need to enjoy being who we are created to be. You could never be a better someone else. Second is nothing; copy is a waste. Being you is the only thing there is to aspire to. Like the fish, I believe there is a location for all graces we have been given. You will do well to find your location, and fulfill staying there.

A man could be many things but not anything better than that for which he is created. If so be that there is something at which one is considered best, why spend so much time on something at which one is less than good? Isn't that a waste of humanity? Sadly, this is where a lot of people spend the most of their lives, on something other than that for which they have been divinely wired.

If you find your purpose, stay with it. You will be like a fish in the waters with it; like a bird on the tree with it; it will be all great. Even if that purpose comes with all the intricacies and challenges, they will be stuff you deal with far less strenuously because of the grace that accompanies you divinely.

CAST DOWN EXCUSES

Oh! And I've met people who will not do things they really ought to be doing because they have reasons why it couldn't be done. They are the set of people I dread to meet. They have every reason why that thing couldn't be done. You will do well to stay away from such persons. Excuses are just cheap escapes from our fulfillment. Jordan Belfort said, "The only thing standing between you and your goal is the bullshit story you keep telling yourself as to why you can't achieve it." Nothing beclouds the mind more than excuses. It is the ladder that failures climb their future with. It is the foundation on which failure is built. It is a blessing to failure and a curse to success. It is a window out of performance and a gateway into failure. It is failure.

Excuses come in different forms; the worst of them come in genuine clothing. Would you please find how to do what you need to do, and stop giving reasons why it could not be done? In the words of Steve Maraboli, "We may blame, give reasons, and even have excuses; but in the end, it is an act of cowardice to not follow your dreams." Soren Kierkegaard wrote, "For like poisonous breath over the fields, like a mass of locusts over Egypt, so the swarm of excuses is a general plague, a ruinous infection among men that eats off the sprouts of the eternal."

We could all make excuses all we want, but if all we have been making is excuses, the world will still be without houses to live in, without clothes to wear, without cars to drive, without clean water to drink; the whole world will still be without form. What we enjoy today are the excuses that men damned. If they made excuses, we wouldn't have what they gave us.

Excuses are a disservice to our purpose. There will always be reasons good enough to not do what you should do, but you've got to look those genuine reasons in the eye and damn them, and go on pursuing life to the full. Can you take a flash back to why you didn't do something you really planned for? You had excuses for it. There will always be reasons. The more people know you with excuses, the less they trust that you could ever get anything done. In the words of Criss Jami, "Like crying wolf, if you keep looking for sympathy as a justification for your actions, you will someday be left standing alone when you really need help." Benjamin Franklin warned, "He that is good for making excuses is seldom good for anything else." Stop doing this disservice to yourself. Cast down excuses, start on working out your dreams and fulfilling your purpose. You will do well, much better without those excuses.

6

The Ultimate Purpose

HIS WILL, YOUR WILL

There is such a thing called God's will. Just like there are ways of God that He expects us to follow, there is a will of His in every circumstance that concerns our life, especially of the purpose for which He made us. We must make it our top priority to find out what His will is. Andrew Wormack once said, "You do not accidentally fulfill God's will, you are going to have to find out what God's will for your life is." We, who are in search of our purpose, must take that admonition to heart.

How do I know God's will? That's probably one of the most asked questions when it comes to purpose issues. I am not a theologian, but I have common understanding. There is God's will revealed in God's word. As a matter of fact, one of the ways to test if what you are considering is God's will is to check with His word, to know whether your thoughts align with His word. What if the Word does not explicitly state that I should choose this over that, or pursue this career instead of that? We have the spirit of God if we are His. And His spirit is the candle that lights our heart. He will direct us; we only need to learn to follow. He will speak to us; we only need to learn to listen. Our loving Father will never leave us without direction.

He speaks in the quietness of our hearts through His still small voice. He speaks to us through His chosen servants whether they are called prophets or pastors. He speaks to us through dreams, visions, and insights. He speaks to us through circumstances around us, and through the experiences of others. By His leading, He guides our hearts and causes us to be attracted to certain purposes that He has for our lives. By the loss of desire that we have, by the dissatisfaction that we feel about something and the feeling that we have to do something about it, by our loss or lack of peace God may be redirecting our hearts and telling us this is not what He wants for us.

There is something He placed in us, even though He gave us freewill to choose our lives' path, that thing is called conscience. It is the check of our freewill. You know when freedom is not tamed it becomes bondage. God planted that red light in us, and if we will just listen and obey His leading through that, I tell you, we will save ourselves a lot of troubles. But that's not man's way.

Man's own way always seems very attractive. If we ignore to follow all the provision He has made to direct us, we will be exactly in our own way, led by our own desires. Wormack said, "You don't do your own things and pray God to bless it – He already blessed what He told you to do." Does that shock you? I guess not. God does not bless what He did not commission. Wherewith will He be able to do that? It'll contravene His word. In the book, *The Life God Blesses*, Gordon MacDonald wrote: "The ill that He blesses is good but unblest good is ill". It's just blessed to find that will and follow. You cannot know better, and He cannot have a worse plan for you than you do for yourself.

Sure, it is possible that what you are doing already, even without having taken time to commune with God over it, is God's will. It is possible that you are already doing what you should be doing according to His will; I still recommend you talk to Him about it. It is not all good ideas that are God ideas. In doing all good things, you might be leaving out the very great thing in His sight that He wants you to do. If you already found out and are doing it, congratulations, there are not many like you, so keep doing it. He blesses what He commissions.

CREATED FOR HIS PURPOSE

The thought of fulfilling purpose strikes, or should strike a chord in the heart of every man, or so I thought until I started encountering people who live just for every passing day. They care less whether there be, by chance, any reason for which they have the life in them. As far as they can get by each day, then they are doing just fine. But are they really that fine? My guess is as good as yours.

The world is bedeviled with many ills, and if people will do no more to add to what obtains right now, the world will still suffer greatly, but hardly will man fold his arms. The greater good of men do no more good to themselves than they do to their environment.

For whatever reason, people hate people and so they do their environment. Even if they do not state it, which they hardly do anyway, by the things that they do, or don't, people feature in news for all sort of reasons having to do with what ill they have brought the world, and, beautiful people in beautiful dresses and apparels hold a job that makes them tell ugly news always. Some news channels are renowned for telling bad news. Good news never makes it to their headlines or breaking news. As a matter of fact, every time you tune into radio or TV for news, you're likely to hear bad news maybe ninety percent of the time, and so it is really depressing to listen to news these days.

More than a year ago, while I was yet compiling materials for this book, a young man of about twenty-one named Dylan Roof in Charleston, South Carolina showed up on the TV as breaking news. What he did? He entered a black populated church in that city and shot nine of the worshipers dead. Their offence? "You've raped our women, and you are taking over the country. I have to do what I have to do. " About a year after in the month of June 2016, the deadliest hate attack by a single gunman happened. A man named Omar Mateen, an American citizen of Afghan origin attacked a nightclub and that event left about fifty people dead, and some fifty-three others injured. His is the more recent of that type as at the time of writing this book, but sure not the only as most Americans and indeed other people in the world will testify that the tendency for hate attacks is not limited to Dylan or Omar. Dylan, Omar and indeed all of us could really do much more to better our environment or at least do no more to add to the damage it is currently suffering.

The curse of poverty could literally be seen, and the stench smelt from a distance when one visits some countries of the world, especially places with high population density. If you have food on your table, and you complain about not having meat, or you have clothes to wear to cover your nakedness and you complain about not having enough shoes to complement, you have shelter – a roof over your head and complain about having an old mattress, you need a lesson in gratitude. Some of the really poor people in some of these places would be uncontrollably thankful just to have a pint of your blessings. Some of these experiences are too graphic to be true.

And there are multitudes of different exposures and experiences, of different climes and countries of the world than my pen can capture. In the heart of these people, there will be no debate, I guess, if I say, purpose does not mean a thing. By chance, and by some act of God, you'll find some of these people who find purpose and live it out. You, my friend, who has the privilege of reading this book right now, to you, fulfillment of purpose is more than just a statement.

YOU WERE CREATED...

The curse of undiscovered purpose is that it leaves one with sour taste of unfulfillment in life. Many a time, one looks at himself and asks the ineschewable question: Am I really worth anything? Is my life worth living? If you find yourself in such despondent state today, I'll like to tell you that you are worth much more than you ever know.

I know this sound like some pep talk but nothing is truer. You were created; you are not an accidental occurrence. You did not just show up on the scene of life without a trace. You were planned for. God planned for you to be here. Even if you are doing all you could possibly do to put your background right out of your mind, you still have a source that produced you. You were formed creatively. Oh! One of my favorite scriptures is that which says: I am wonderfully and fearfully made. My friend, you are not an accident. It took at least nine months for your gestation, that's not hasty. Even if the union that begot you was illegitimate, that's as far as it goes. You are not illegitimate. You are not a bastard. You have a father who created you and planned for you to be here. You are an expression of His ingenuity; you are a display of His artistic creative prowess, a manifestation of His splendor, the crowning of His glory. The way producers look at the beauty of what they have made and are proud to show them off is nothing compared to how your Creator wants to show you off.

Even if your mother did all she could to abort you as a fetus, that you eventually came to this world tells a lot about the preciousness and worth of your life – it couldn't be taken, not even by drugs. You were formed, you were made, you were created; the Master Craftsman Himself made you. How dare you look down on yourself – the product of the maker of heaven and earth? It is an aberration, an effusion of ignorance of the components that went into making you that makes you look down on yourself. You could never take the time to understand what it costs the Creator to make you if you keep looking down on yourself.

You are unique in yourself and truly no one like you. You are probably saying to yourself: he couldn't be talking about me. Well, I am talking about you. Yes, you who feel so unworthy because of what you have done wrong. You who feel so inadequate because of what life may have thrown at you. You who feel so incapable because of the many failures you have recorded in your life and what people have said are impossible to achieve by you. You are the best there is. There could never be another you, only a redefined you. Your height, your weight, complexion and all you have are part of your design. Black is beautiful, common, fair is great, but none like you. You may not belong to the class of those people around you call beautiful, you may not be as educated as the people that are revered because of their advantages in life, but I put it to you that you could never wish to be anyone else, because you'd never be good enough a copy of anyone. You are unique, uniquely created. The mold that was used in forming you was made solely for you, that's why anyone wanting to be like you can only at best be a copy. Never feel worthless, never put yourself down, you were created by God.

Some people have a habit of making you feel inadequate, say to those, enough! If you don't put yourself down, you cannot continue to allow others to do that to you. You don't have to be in a relationship that places no value on you. Are you friends or acquaintance with anyone who makes you feel worthless? You know some people take pleasure in that? How much more can you endure? The time comes when you stamp your feet and stick to your guns, and that time is now. Reintroduce yourself to yourself, and to them. Let them know that you know who you are, and you are drawing a line on how much more you can take.

Just remember that it all starts with you. If you keep putting yourself down, you put yourself in no better position for others to address you. If you hold yourself up high, they'll have to respect that or stay out of your life. You will have to confess, and repeat to yourself every day like you are in danger of forgetting it, that you are the gift of God to your world, you are the effulgence of His morning, you are resplendent in the covering of His glory, you are a sure bet of His excellence, you are unique specie, God's own heritage, apex of His invention.

If you find something in you that the Maker didn't put there – a lifestyle that He did not commission you to live, a desire He warns you to stay off of, a habit that's not contained in your Standard Operating Procedure, a tare sown among your wheat, a reflection of Satan's destructive tendencies, you'll have to cooperate with the Creator to take it away. You cannot afford to put on yourself what He does not empower you for. You are His creature my friend, you were created…

…FOR SOMETHING

The thought on your mind perhaps is "the picture you are painting is not a reflection of me. You don't know what I'm going through. You don't even know how terrible I feel each day I wake up." I acknowledge that your situation is dire, I agree that you don't even wish same for your enemies. I may not know how it feels or the details of your travails, but I have a word for you: you are not alone. There might not be many people like you going through your turmoil, but I assure you, you are not the only one. That word comes with a promise because God is faithful. He will not put more on you than you can bear.

How incredible!

You probably did not know how strong you are, by His grace, until you were confronted with that predicament. You did not know the stuff you were made of until life asked of you a show of that strength. You did not know how much grace you have at your disposal until you had a situation that placed a demand on that grace. The Amplified Version of Isaiah 41:10 says "…I will strengthen and harden you to difficulties, yes I will help you…" that is God letting you know that you cannot be overcome by that situation. Be it sickness in your body, a bloodline curse you are battling with, you are overdue for marriage yet no one stops by, you are married without a child in years and with marital pressures arising therefrom, you are faced with an unfaithful spouse, your in-laws are the least you pray to meet, your job is a nightmare, your children are not giving you peace, your pocket needs redemption, your life lacks meaning or is even being threatened, your church is far from what you thought it was, your friends are all gone, your education is bleeding red ink, your project is stalled, your business is in comatose, you lost a loved one, nothing is working… whatever it is, He assures that you will not be consumed by it. If you cooperate with God and do His bidding, He declares "when you pass through the waters, I will be with you; and through the rivers, they shall not overwhelm you; when you walk through fire you shall not be burned, and the flame shall not consume you." (Isa. 43:2 ESV). God does not betray His word; He is too faithful to fail you.

You may be going through worse situations than I have described above, but no matter for how long it has defied solutions, I submit to you that it is not permanent. It is a temporary affliction and it is not worthy to be compared with the glory that shall be revealed in you. I do not know conclusively all things, but the good Lord does, and His word says so.

Despite all the odds that you are confronted with, you must keep your eye on your purpose – on that, for which you are created. When the challenges are gone, the purpose remains. Your negative experience is a distraction from your purpose; you cannot afford to take your eyes off of that something you were created for.

You are so unique in your creation that I believe the mold used in making you is not available to be used for someone else. Your fingerprints, your palm lines, tongue prints and even your mind works differently from others. Do you want to know? There is no second you! That's how unique you are. And in your uniqueness, the Creator Himself made sure that there are things only you could do, thoughts only you could think, things only you could create the way you do them. Do you know that there are countless lives invariably waiting for such things that you could do? There are lives attached to you. In fulfilling your purpose for coming into this world, you enhance theirs as well.

Now don't give me that look. You cannot afford not to be that someone or to do that something you were created to do. You will not only fail yourself, you will fail others as well. You don't want to live beyond usefulness and only in old age, perhaps in old people's homes, before you begin to regret that, there are books you should have written, songs you should have written, sang or produced, clothing lines you should have created, cars you should have designed, furniture you should have made, businesses you should have started, inventions you should not die with, people you should have helped, communities you should have impacted, homes you should have helped, children you should have helped raise well, loved ones or family you did not do enough to be with… the list is inexhaustible. In the words of Greenleaf Whittier, "if the saddest words are 'it might have been' the next saddest have to be 'I should have tried'." You were created for something, you cannot not want to be that thing.

There is a purpose in you that's crying out daily for fulfillment. You hear the sound as you go to your job every day, you hear the sound as you try to console yourself with other cares that really matter less. The terrible thing is that the voice of purpose gets louder as you age, and draw nearer to the end of life. The decibels of that sound tune louder a unit per time of life, such that, early in life, you are searching for, listening for that sound, and even though it's there, it's in its still small volume. You fight to hear it. But in old age, it is so loud you could hear it, so real you could feel it, so near you could touch it but it's far gone you could hardly attain it. Of course, you don't want to wait until that time that's why you are searching now for it.

I believe that everyone is created for a mission – a particular mission in life. We must not go through life not finding out what it is. Even if you are so hugely talented that you could do almost everything, there is that purpose you were created for, that, in doing other things, if you don't do that one, you will hardly be fulfilled at the end. And that's quite the confusion between talent and life's purpose.

7

The Purpose Tests

HOW DO I KNOW WHAT I SHOULD BE DOING WITH MY LIFE?

This ought to be the first deep self-examining question anyone is really asking themselves. This book wouldn't have been necessary if there was no such question. And if anyone could answer that question, they have half-solved the challenges of purpose fulfillment in life. In the words of Laverne Cox, "Each and every one of us has a purpose in this world that is endowed upon us from a power greater than ourselves."

If the first question to ask is: How do I know what I should be doing with my life? Then the next question ought to be: How do I know if I'm already doing what I should be doing with my life? Because, I am almost certain that anyone asking that first question is already doing something – something they consider important, something they probably even think is their purpose in life, but they just need to hear someone say, that's it. As you may have already discovered, that's certainly not a statement most people hear. That statement is why you are reading this book probably. Okay, let's reverse it. Let's say that statement has been made before you ever got to searching for your purpose. If you find that, the Creator already said, "That's it," what will you choose to do to match that acceptance? If the life you will choose to live already has the pass mark on it, what will that life be?

Many a people will live most of their lives seeking answers to this question. Sometimes some of us are already doing what we are supposed to be doing with our lives without knowing it. Some people are already using their gift or one of their gifts and are getting celebrated all over, they just are not certain, when they are by themselves whether what they are is what they should always be.

We all at least deserve to know whether what we are doing is what we should be doing. We all deserve to be certain that we are on track to destiny fulfillment. We deserve to know whether if we are to meet our Creator now, we would be bold to tell Him, I did on earth what You sent me there to do. We all deserve to know. To be honest with you, only a paltry few can tell that they are doing what they should be doing. How do we know whether we are already part of the few? Let us examine together in the next few pages the various tests that we may apply to help validate our claim or clear our doubts. I have to warn that this is in no way an exhaustive approach, the ultimate is what the Creator tells you, but these will help a lot to convince that you heard the Creator or not.

THE JOY TEST

The words 'joy' and 'happiness' are oft used interchangeably; I might not do anything different here. In fact, I might add the word 'enthusiasm' to the synonyms.

According to Psalms sixteen verse eleven, when you are shown the path of life, you will find fullness of joy. The joy that is implied here is not just that which comes as a result of expected results coming through. It is not because you have your hopes achieved. Of course, you must rejoice when your plans are achieved but even the least enthusiastic of people rejoices at that. The point here is, you are happy in what you do, whether that thing gives immediate or eventual good results. The wisest man that ever lived said in Ecclesiastes chapter two verse ten, that his heart rejoiced in all his labor.

Do you have joy doing what you call your life's purpose? Are you happy going to that job every day? Are you enthusiastic that that thing you are doing is what you are doing? Are you happy not because of the pay or of any other benefits that the work gives you, but because that work brings you pleasure – it soothes your purpose? If the pay and other benefits are taken away from that job, will it still be what you are doing? Could joy or happiness be the only reason you are working? If you always sold your joy for what comes at the end of thirty days, I tell you, the time comes when you can no longer do that. The contest between your pay and your conscience becomes obvious your pay can't win. If you consistently ignore the trump of conscience, love letter to frustration is written, signed, sealed and delivered.

Several times when we have loss of joy or feel a dire dissatisfaction with what we are doing, it could mean that we are not doing what we ought to be doing in the first place. You want to check again, I guess. Do you have joy doing what you are doing? Because nothing compares to the joy you feel when you do what you are purposed to be doing. Purpose is reached when what brings us our deepest joy meets the needs of others.

THE LOVE TEST

There's probably something you could hardly get tired of doing. Something you just fall in love with doing that you could do until your last breath. And I am not talking about frivolities, I am talking about life's purpose – a work or service you could devote your entirety to whether it be salvaging situations, developing problem-solving programmes, attending to people's health, teaching children, writing, fine arts, singing, working in the laboratory or workshop, anything at all that is destiny-prone.

I once heard of a public speaker, a renowned one in Nigeria, whom if you met outside of the stage would hardly say more than a few sentences. He's a man of few words indeed. But if you met him on the stage or in a training session, he could spend the whole day talking. When you find what you love to do, you'll need no prodding to do it.

Ask most people who are fulfilling purpose, they love what they do. If not for love, they'd have stopped doing it. I assure you, all of them have had enough reasons to. Maybe you are doing something you find difficult to stop, it has nothing to do with what you get or don't get from that thing, it has all to do with what you attach to that thing that money cannot buy.

Do you love your work? Do you love the fact that your work helps solve the problems that it solves? Do you love that you are involved with doing something that takes care of other people's problems? Do you even love the fact that you are identified by that work you do? If status were to be taken out of that job, would you still be doing it?

THE CONFIDENCE TEST

It is amusing when people get cowed in when they see other people in their own fields. If you are so ashamed of what you do, you should doubt whether it is your purpose in life. A welding technician feels inadequate when he sees a lawyer; a sanitation officer feels low when he sees a medical doctor; and so on. We all need each other. That profession you think so lowly of makes people's living possible, and in the eye of purpose, no one profession is greater than the other. We are the ones who make our professions, our professions don't make us. I will never forget how the late Isaac Durojaiye alias Otunba Gadaffi made the *Shit* business in Nigeria big. The man handled people's convenience needs, cleared their sewages, provided them with mobile toilets and got wealthy doing that. He was said to have made over seven hundred million naira doing the *shit* business. He traveled the world and sat on tables with presidents, kings, and queens doing *shit* business. He is widely known for saying stuff like, "*Shit money no dey smell*". He was so proud of what he was doing, he got several thousands of youths empowered doing same. His purpose was simple: sanitation. How much can you boast of what you are doing? How confident are you talking about what you do?

In the congregation of other people, you will be able to hold your head up high, and never feel low if you follow the path of life, if you are doing the bidding of destiny. You may not have started out knowing that you should be proud of your life's purpose, but as soon as it clicks in your spirit, your confidence swells and you are not ashamed of it. As a matter of fact, out the window goes non-confidence. And when someone asks you, what do you do? You can tell them, "I am a street sweeper," looking at them in the eye.

THE HUNGER TEST

I might as well call this the 'thirst' test. For the food you love to eat, I guess you hardly get tired having it more than once per day. Those who have become addicted to certain drinks or soda make efforts to not remember how many bottles they have had so they will not be discouraged, sadly, people are not comparably hungry about fulfilling their purpose in life.

What are you so hungry for? Which profession or function are you so thirsty for? What do you never get tired of having?

What is your life's purpose? How frantically do you pursue to achieve it? How much do you fight to do something about it daily? How often do you do anything to move you closer to becoming the best in that line of your purpose? How often are you in competition with yourself about what you call your destiny?

Yea I know you are busy working – on other people's destiny. Do you ever set time aside to attend to yours daily? If you say you are a writer, how many chapters of the book you have been writing for the past one year have you completed? If you say your life's purpose is to sing, which of your songs have you recorded? Have you been hungry enough to do something about your purpose, yet?

Because if it is your purpose, your hunger for it will be natural; you will desire more of, to do more of, to relate more with, to know more of, to spend more time on, etc. this desire will be there in your heart, you will always long for your purpose.

What you do currently, do you hunger to do more of it? Is there something else that you rather hunger and thirst for? Is there some profession, work or discipline you know if you get your hands on, you could hardly want to do something else? Is there something you yearn for so badly? Is there some activity that you desire to always do? Could that activity be your purpose?

THE KNOWLEDGE TEST

This is related to the hunger test above. Knowledge is power they say. One who knows something is empowered about that thing, and what you don't know, you are not greater than. How much do you know about your purpose generally, and what it'll take you to fulfill it specifically? How many people who are into similar fields have you spoken to? How many books about your purpose have you read? How many seminars/workshops have you attended? How many mentors do you have? Do you even know of anyone who is doing it? How many of the above are you planning to do to bring you closer to fulfilling that purpose? How eager are you to know more on a daily basis about what you ultimately represent? This test is both of what you know, and desire to know.

A wise man once said: there is no difference between those who cannot read and those who will not read, they are all illiterates. At least as it concerns what they do not know anything about.

There must be some knowledge that attracts you. Besides being naturally inquisitive about things, you will find that your inquisitiveness is more towards some kind of knowledge, and whenever you have opportunity to know more about that thing, meet someone in that field or anything that brings you close to that form of knowledge; it always seems you can't wait. You are certainly attracted to that knowledge and you need to think a little more about it and be certain why it is like that.

The reason you read certain books rather than others is probably because of this same reason. The reason certain kinds of news get your attention while others just swat past your ears is because of the same reason. The reason you are engaged in certain kind of discussion with certain kind of people is because of this same reason. Have you found out what you really always desire to know more of; something about which you are never tired of learning? That thing perhaps stands tall among other forms of knowledge of other things that you know, and could be a pointer to your purpose.

THE GRACE TEST

As you have read already in this course of this book, whatever your purpose is, you are already graced for it. There is a supernatural ability that has been given to you already. You may not have discovered it but that in no way negates that you have it. In your purpose, you operate naturally without much struggle. Have you found what that thing is, that you do with ease, that you don't have to struggle to do? What comes naturally to you? Where are you more at home, more like a fish in the river? Where is your area of natural grace – the area where you hardly trained yet perform near excellence?

It is not arrogance to say you are good at something. I think rather that it is annoying to not acknowledge that you are good at something. If you are good, you are good. It is your grace. You owe no apologies to anyone for being so good. However, you must also acknowledge that you are good while being humble at it – Someone graced you for it.

There is no one who hasn't been graced at something. It could be talking, making people comfortable, sharing jokes, counseling people, teaching people to understand rather complex things, aptitude to solve rather difficult questions, resolving conflicts, having flexible bodies to twist in gymnastics, having swift feet to outpace anyone on track with you in a race, organizing events, attractive and charming smiles, doing craft and repairing almost anything mechanical or electronic, having insight into how other people think or perceive issues, dancing, cooking, baking, constructing, making designs that sit just right on people, and on and on.

Have you found where you are so graced, abundantly graced that even you acknowledge it as well as other people do? You need to know that these graces are not given to you for the fun of it, there is a purpose for it. You should find further whether that is exactly your purpose.

THE OBSESSION TEST

When I begin to work on a book or prepare for a speaking engagement, my day is not complete when I have not penned down something or given some kind of attention to that. As a matter of fact, I'd always say I've not worked today as if the whole day depended on what I do or don't do on these projects. I sleep and wake up thinking about what else to do. I get easily obsessed with these kinds of projects. Let's apply same to the quest for purpose. If we can be so consumed with passion about our lives' purpose as we sometimes get with transient projects, we could really make our lives a perpetual project, and how awesome that would be.

The reason for which we are created could become so consuming that we could hardly get sleep without it; we could sleep, wake, eat, drink, and live it; our entire lives could become summed up in it. As a matter of fact, sleep for us becomes a reward for the well-done job of the day. And there is no harm in it at all. As a matter of fact, we'd rather that our lives be summed up in our purpose because that is us, every other thing is not nearly as important.

How consumed with passion are you with that thing which represents purpose to you? I mean, is there a kind of activity or mission you are really obsessed about, that you could commit your life to? How obsessed are you with the path you are toeing? How much of yourself are you giving to it every other day of your life? Some or all of yourself? Could there be something else you could give? Are you always looking forward to giving it more? Are you consumed with it? Can your life be summed up in it?

Obsession is the reason you don't want to do something else. The reason why people know you with one thing and that thing only is because of your obsession with it. And there is something that you can get easily obsessed by. Not a distraction, but a life's purpose. The obsession is the reason why you are always seeking improved way of delivering on that same work, and getting better at it. So, what is that thing that you could become obsessed by? Have you found it yet?

THE CAPACITY TEST

If you look at your life's purpose, and you have the capacity immediately to accomplish it, you probably should look further. Your purpose cannot possibly be so cheap you could fund it. God always gives us more to do in life than we have in our pocket to fund. Don't get me wrong. There is a natural, nay, supernatural ability that God gave to man at creation that makes the fulfillment of life at maximum level very possible. God gave man so much at creation that most men return more than a few to Him when they die. Yes, we are so richly blessed. But, hardly does any man truly know his true capacity; everyone just takes life headlong. Life is more a process than a destination; it is in fulfilling one thing that we become confident to take on another, most times.

But also, if your purpose is involved, you are willing to try it out; to test your capacity. No matter how gargantuan the assignment, you may feel inadequate, but you take on the process, and because it is your purpose, you enjoy the process, even if it doesn't look like you are succeeding in it, you kind of enjoy the lessons that failure teaches you, and you discover better ways of doing it, and will you succeed? You bet. Remember the story of Thomas Edison and his electric light bulb experiment? The umpteenth failure would not come if he stopped, and so wouldn't the light bulb. In reality, times come when you become discouraged, disappointed, disgusted, dismayed, deserted, and all the dis…, that only makes you human. You, I and every other person feel the same, but whatever makes you go back to that duty post, whether you heard someone talked about not giving up, or you thought about not giving up, whatever that thing is, that you heeded is a signal that your capacity calls out for expression.

So, do you have the mental capacity to at least begin the pursuit of that purpose? Do you have the mental currency to pay the deposit for that purpose journey you want to embark on? Are you so intimidated you don't mind a dare? Are you ready to do it afraid? Are you willing to begin again even if you fall and crash in the course of the project? Are you so ready mentally to take on the process giving it all it takes until you arrive at your destination? What is that thing about which you are ready? What is that thing you are building your capacity on? What is that thing that you are developing yourself for? Does it look like what you could spend the rest of your life chasing after?

THE CONNECTION TEST

One of my favorite verses in the Holy Scriptures is that which says the deep calls unto the deep. That phrase is capable of several interpretations, and has been interpreted severally but the interpretation that soothes my analysis here is this: when you find something about your purpose around you, the purpose in you longs to connect with it – the deep in you calls out to the deep outside you.

Have you observed yourself enough to find that you get angry at how some things around you are done, and you really know you could do them better? Have you discovered that you are always wishing you had the opportunity to better what you see? What is that thing that happens around you, and you really long for? What do you feel a connection to? Is there perhaps someone you watch on the TV or stage and you feel you could do the same thing you are watching? Is there a book you are reading and you feel you could write? Is there a piece of cloth you are wearing or see someone wearing and you feel you could design better? Do you see people's make-up, and you feel you could do better? Let me tell you what I heard someone say one day: "If you refuse to write that book, someday you will read it. If you refuse to design that cloth, someday you will buy it. If you refuse to create that recipe, one day you will go to a restaurant and eat it. Whatever your purpose is that you refuse to carry out, someone else will, and you will pay for it." That is food for thought.

There is always a connection in us to something outside of us that resembles our purpose, what is that thing for you? Look for it, it is there. If you seek, you will find. You will find something done, and you are saying to yourself, I can do that too, that's what I should be doing. Go on, free yourself, that deep in you is calling out to the deep outside of you, let it out, listen to yourself, pay attention to what you are paying attention to, and that could just be your purpose you are looking at.

More of this in chapter nine.

THE PURPOSE- REASONS TEST

We all do things for different reasons and intentions. Sometimes we just feel like it, sometimes necessity is laid on us, sometimes we are overtaken with emotions, some other times it is just our habits that lead us to do those things, and yet other times, because we see others doing those things we also do it. We do different things for different reasons.

But maybe you have stopped to ask yourself before: Why am I doing this stuff? Quite honestly, you can assure yourself, and anyone that cares to know that you did not do what you did for self-seeking gains; it was nothing about you, you just couldn't resist doing that thing. Now we have to be clear that I am not talking about doing just anything. I am talking about things that apply to life's assignment, add value to humanity and bring God praise. I am talking about purpose-leading tendencies. Is the pleasure of that activity helping you to reach your ultimate invaluable happiness, helping to give your life a meaning, beating your life into shape, and making you desire to do more for such positive reasons.

If you would take money, fame, self-seeking glory and other trappings away from that activity, would you still be doing it? Are you in it for the greater good? One way to know that is to subject that activity to the test of time. Without all these trappings, if after a reasonable time, years, you still do what you do, there might be a purpose green light there.

If you read the story of Martin Luther Jnr of the US, Mahatma Gandhi of India, Gani Fawehinmi of Nigeria, and Nelson Mandela of South Africa, you will find one thing common among them. They all were given to pursuing the course of others, and they did, not because of what they might get from it. Not the fame, glory or any of the self-seeking motives that we see today. That someone will rise up for the sake of others in the unique ways that each of them did; purpose led them there.

What are you doing? And why are you doing it? Could it be that purpose is leading you or you are leading yourself or others are leading you or self-seeking gain is leading you? The best answer could be a 'no' to all the above, and 'I don't know' to purpose. If you can strip your self from yourself, what's left might be your purpose.

8

Purpose Navigation System

It was in the early days when the devices came pre-installed on cars. I'd never truly seen that before except on certain geographic devices. I know I have read about it, but maybe I couldn't connect between what I have read and what was like a digital map before me, except that this map had arrows of different colors indicating even the hotels, shops and all landmark points along the street. I had just seen my first dashboard navigation system.

To navigate is to find a way through a place, or direct the course of something according to the Encarta dictionaries. It also means to follow a correct or satisfactory course along a route. Those definitions clearly encapsulate what this chapter is about. You are hoping to get some navigation for your life, isn't that why you are reading this book anyway?

I checked up navigation system in Wikipedia.org, and this is what I got:

A navigation system is a (usually electronic) system that aids in navigation. (By the way, to navigate means to find a way through a place or to direct the course of something or someone). Navigation systems may be entirely on board a vehicle or vessel, or they may be located elsewhere and communicate via radio or other signals with a vehicle or vessel, or they may use a combination of these methods.

Navigation systems may be capable of:

- containing maps, which may be displayed in human readable format via text or in a graphical format

- determining a vehicle or vessel's location via sensors, maps, or information from external sources

- providing suggested directions to a human in charge of a vehicle or vessel via text or speech

- providing directions directly to an autonomous vehicle such as a robotic probe or guided missile

- providing information on nearby vehicles or vessels, or other hazards or obstacles

- providing information on traffic conditions and suggesting alternative directions

That is what the free encyclopedia said.

Now, let us replace a few words used there with the ones that really matter to our discussion here. Let us replace the words "navigation" with "purpose navigation", the words "vehicle", "vessel" with the words "human" or "person", the word "electronic" with the word "divine", the word "radio" with the word "spirit", the word "traffic" with "life", and the words "such as" with the words "just like" and edit a few other parts of that text. See how that looks below:

A purpose navigation system is a (usually divine) system that aids in navigation. The navigation systems may be entirely in a human or person, or they may be located elsewhere and communicate via spirit or other life's signals with a human or person, or they may use a combination of these methods.

Purpose Navigation systems may be capable of:

- containing life's maps, which may be displayed in human readable format via text or in a graphical format

- determining a human or person's location via sensors, maps, or information from both internal and external sources

- providing suggested directions to one in charge of a human or person via text or speech

- providing directions directly to a person just like a robotic probe or guided missile

- providing information on nearby humans or persons, or other hazards or obstacles

- providing information on life's conditions and suggesting alternative directions,

And let's add this:

- providing direction to man, and helping him to find his way in life.

And I think that quite applies to everyone on earth. I believe every individual's got a map designed for their lives. And that is not something they determine for themselves. That is something divinely given to guide their lives.

The Global Positioning System (GPS) is a type of navigation system. It is a network of about 30 satellites orbiting the earth at an altitude of 20,000km. And according to physics.org, wherever you are on the planet, at least four GPS satellites are visible at any time. Each one transmits information about its position and the current time at regular intervals. These signals traveling at the speed of light are intercepted by your GPS receiver, which calculates how far away each satellite is based on how long it took for the messages to arrive. With the GPS tracking software, therefore, our smartphones, digital maps, dashboard navigation maps and other smart devices can receive information in whatever form and place.

To know that scientists could make inventions that map and guide our vehicles, devices and all that, and to think that God who created us left us without guidance in life is foolhardy. God has not created the man in whose life He has no interest. He has not created the man about whom He does not care even if he goes missing. He has not created the man who should wander and have no direction and since He has completed His creation, then He may never create such a man. Your life is mapped. It is not to be lived the way you want it. There is a guide for your life. There is a map for you. There is a sensor in you that receives the signal from the satellite that guides your life, and wherever you are, at whatever time, in whatever situation, that satellite never ceases to transmit signal, question is: Is your sensor still on? Is your GPS software still active receiving signal from the satellite over your life?

What are the types of Purpose Navigation Systems that direct the course of our lives?

THE WORD

When a manufacturer makes a product, he will not always be there to guide the user of the product. To avoid confusion about the product use, he attaches a manual to that product giving instructions to the user. The manual attached to our lives is the bible – the word of God. This is not religion. It is a guide for living. The first purpose GPS. The earlier anyone embraced the word, the sooner the person finds the purpose for living. The word in Psalms One hundred and nineteen verse One hundred and five, says, "Thy word is a lamp unto my feet and a light unto my path." (KJV). What does a lamp do? It gives light. And why do we need light especially in the darkness of life? Psalm thirty-seven verse thirty-one answers that "The law of their God is in their hearts; their feet do not slip." To maintain firmness in the journey of life, one must retain the word of God in him.

The word does not only provide light and firmness in the purpose trip of life, it also guarantees prosperity and success in the pursuit of it. How would you like it that upon obedience to instructions, your life's purpose is not only discovered, it is fulfilled? Joshua, the second in command in the Mosaic army, said in chapter one verse eight of his book: "This book of the law shall not depart from your mouth, but you shall meditate on it day and night, so that you may be careful to do according to all that is written in it. For then you will make your way prosperous, and then you will have good success" (ESV). I like that part that guarantees prosperity and success.

The challenge with us most times is that we just want to rationalize things. We just want to depend on our reasoning to get through life. We do not consider the limits of rationalization. We have failed to realize that there is a limit to what our high-capacity brains can give us. We have soon forgotten that Someone created that brain we are depending solely on. Wouldn't it be more rewarding if we are able to connect with the One who created the gray matter? Don't we realize that this life did not start here on this earth? Don't we realize that there is a spirit realm which controls the earth realm, and we must refer to that spirit to get the best out of the earth?

In case you are wondering why so much emphasis on the word, take a look at this instruction Moses gave by the hand of God to the Israelites as recorded in Deuteronomy chapter six verses six to nine:

> *And these words, which I command thee this day, shall be in thine heart:* (and not just for you alone)

> *And thou shalt teach them diligently unto thy children, and shalt talk of them when thou sittest in thine house, and when thou walkest by the way, and when thou liest down, and when thou risest up.* (just in case you think that's enough)

> *And thou shalt bind them for a sign upon thine hand, and they shall be as frontlets between thine eyes.* (now take it further)

> *And thou shalt write them upon the posts of thy house, and on thy gates.* (KJV, all emphasis mine)

Today, by His Spirit, the words are in our hearts, and we could just look in, and find them there. They become the compass, the first thereof, which helps to navigate our way. Our lives are mapped by the word, and if we look in our lives and can't find the word, we are like a stranger who has lost the compass for his way. We could keep going around in circles, for as long as we refuse to check in the word, we will never find the right purpose for our lives.

You might be asking, does the word say I am to be a doctor, lawyer, musician, mathematician, writer, or any such profession? No, certainly no. The word said much more than that. The word said exactly why you are created, and it is in fulfilling the main purpose for which you are created, that you find the profession that tags along. You were created ultimately to show forth His glory. Check in the word and see it for yourself.

You might be wondering, what about the person I might even marry? Does the word say Mary is for me Joseph, Maxwell for me Sandra, Bisi for me Chukwudi, Aisha for me Dania or Tracey for me Bill? It's the same like I said above. Someone will tag along in the journey of life, the word does not state who for you, but it gives you a guide on who should be for you.

You will always need to return to the Word Himself as you go along. You cannot understand and follow the word if you don't relate to the One who's behind it. It is this relationship that just connects the dots for you, and help you to know if music it is or law, or if Mary it is or Maxwell. Read the word, relate with the Word Himself.

As it is for careers and relationships, so it is for everything that concerns our entire lives. We must work under the guidance of the word to set foot on the proper path of life.

PRAYER

Prayer is amazing. Everyone prays eventually. Whether you believe in Jesus Christ as the Way, or you seek spirituality through other religion or the worship of other gods, you pray. It is like Victor, a wise man, once said,

"Certain thoughts are prayers. There are moments when, whatever be the attitude of the body, the soul is on its knees." I have heard stories of some people who claim to not believe in any god and just believe that life is whatever you make of it. And I have heard of times when such people find themselves in sudden danger, like a motor accident, or the danger of fire or of a gunman who held them hostage shooting others as he approaches them. And the only thing that came out of the mouth of such people is "Jesus!" or "God please save me". They may not have been conscious of it, but they just prayed... to the God.

The wisest man that ever lived counseled in the book of Proverbs chapter three verses five to seven, that, you should:

> *Trust in the LORD with all thine heart, and lean not unto thine own understanding.*
>
> *In all thy ways acknowledge him, and he shall direct thy paths.*
>
> *Be not wise in thine own eyes...* (KJV)

His father, King David had earlier declared in Psalms chapter thirty-seven verse twenty-three that:

> *The steps of a good man are ordered by the LORD: and he delighteth in his way.* (KJV)

One of the greatest prophets that ever lived also said in Jeremiah chapter ten verse twenty-three:

> *O LORD, I know that the way of man is not in himself: it is not in man that walketh to direct his steps.* (KJV)

Mother Teresa had this to say, "Prayer is not asking. Prayer is putting oneself in the hands of God, at His disposition, and listening to His voice in the depth of our hearts."

We cannot, as it were, direct our own lives as it concerns making major destiny-related decisions. If our lives depend on God, we are going to have to trust Him to direct us. Besides, who knows more about a product than the one who manufactured it? We are His creation and should depend on Him for direction. The Lord knows the very end of our lives even before we began living it. How then do we talk to that God except in prayers? How do we receive His directions for our lives when we refuse to pray? How will He guide us, when He can't hear us asking for His guidance?

Some think that God will automatically guide their lives because they are created by Him. You might as well expect to just get a job because you are now a graduate without applying for it or just walk up to Nigeria's Aso rock or the US white house to see the president of those countries just because you are a citizen. And besides, get nothing wrong; God is incomparable with any of these or any other one at all. A man receives nothing, guidance inclusive, who does not ask, and asking is done by praying. Prayer directs. Prayer leads. Prayer guides.

When we pray, God holds our hands together with us, walks us through life, and get us into our purpose. Whether you see His hands on yours or not, as far as you prayed asking for His help, He has His hands on you and will help you.

We should not pre-empt God when we pray. We should not want God to speak to us in particular ways. When we do that, we try to box God. No one can box the Lord. He is the almighty. Sometimes we want Him to speak to us in certain ways, He may have spoken to us already, or is speaking in other ways, but because we didn't get to hear Him the way we wanted to, we conclude that He didn't speak.

Elijah the prophet had a similar experience when he stood upon the mount before the Lord in the book of first Kings chapter nineteen verses eleven and twelve. There was a strong wind that rent the heavens and broke the rocks in pieces, Elijah must have thought, oh! There comes the Lord, but the Lord was not in it. After the wind was an earthquake, and certainly, Elijah must have concluded, let me put myself in order for the Lord has shown up, but the Lord was not in it either. After the quake came a fire, and maybe

Elijah thought since God is a consuming fire, and I've seen what He could do with fire, then surely He has come, but the Lord was not in the fire too. But after the fire came a still small voice, and there it was, the voice of the Lord almighty. Still small voice. It is of us to listen for His voice – whether that be audible, still and small or by simply guiding our minds, whichever way He chooses, we must learn to listen. I think when we pray, we must listen more because prayer as a dialogue must also mean that the Person to whom you talked, talk back to you. I bet you He said something – before, during or after you prayed.

As I wrote this book, I did interact with a couple of people about how they knew God led them into what they were doing. One of them told me how that he thought when he prayed, God will just show up in a dream, or speak into his ears, or direct him to read a portion of the scriptures that explains the answers to his questions, or better still just speak to someone to come talk to him about the whole thing. He even went further to remind God not to be partial because people had testified that God spoke to them audibly about what He had created them to do in life, and his case couldn't be different. Some other people just confided in me that they never heard any voice, nor had any dream, but they just felt that they are to do what they are doing. I bet this is the case with most people. I mean, how many of us really hear God shouting in our ears "My daughter, I have created you to be a medical doctor. Either this or nada." How many? Most of the time, prayer positions our hearts for the guidance of God. He just holds our hands because we have invited Him to, and leads us in our minds by the circumstances around us, the passion we feel, the pain of others that we see, the desire to change something, the joy we derive from doing that thing, the love we have towards that thing or nothing we can even describe and so on.

In praying concerning purpose, another scenario plays up where we are expecting a certain answer. We approach God with a question, but we already have the answer we want to hear in our hearts. Eventually, that is the answer we will hear. We should not go to God with the answers to our questions; otherwise, we did not have a question in the first place. We should not allow our desires to deafen our listening. If the answers that were to come from God do not tally with our preference, then God did not answer, we think. We sometimes think what we want for ourselves is better than what God could want for us. Nothing is more deceptive in the place of prayers.

Balaam the prophet could have lost his head were it not for the sensitivity of his donkey. In Numbers chapter twenty-two, twice he went to the Lord asking the same question until he heard the answer he wanted to hear, and that would just have cost him his life, save for his ass – the colt he rode.

The best answer for us sometimes is "no", and that is just better than "yes" if it comes from the Lord. The best answer for us sometimes is silence, and that is far better than any sound, as far as it is the Lord that kept it. As it concerns purpose, we must learn to hear Him, whichever way He speaks, because that is the best for us.

MEDITATION

I'm quite aware that the word meditation carries different meanings and is used in different contexts, so I'll limit my discussion on it to that which profits us as far as the theme here discussed is concerned.

A dictionary defines meditation as a written or spoken discourse expressing considered thoughts on a subject. Another dictionary defines it as the act of thinking about something carefully, calmly, seriously, and for some time, or an instance of such thinking. It is also defined as the emptying of the mind of thoughts, or the concentration of the mind on one thing, in order to aid mental or spiritual development, contemplation, or relaxation.

Meditation is a purpose navigation system.

The more you think about something, the bigger that thing gets in your mind. Whatever you give thoughts to, you give life to; and the reverse is equally right. If you intend to take life out of something, don't think about it. Things just won't mean much to you if you don't think about them.

God knew the power of meditation so much that upon the assumption of office as the leader of Israel, one of the very first instructions God gave to Joshua was to meditate. In Joshua chapter one verse eight, the word says:

> *This book of the law shall not depart out of your mouth, but you shall meditate on it day and night, that you may observe and do according to all that is written in it. For then you shall make your way prosperous, and then you shall deal wisely and have good success.* (AMP)

The meditation had to be done day and night! There is sure power in meditation.

When we think, we reach into our own souls, and the more we think, the more we dig into it. The mind is a mine, meditation helps to explore it. The soul is a reservoir, meditation helps to fetch from it. Meditation empowers you with the fetcher with which you can constantly reach deep into your own very soul, drink to your fill of the water of life which therein flows. Meditation helps to guide your mind as you engage it, to the very same purpose for which you were created; it helps you to weigh on the scale what really means more to you, and what you'd rather concentrate on. Meditation guides you to know yourself more, and to digest the fullness of your creation. Meditation helps to focus your mind on what you should concentrate your life on.

Have you really engaged in it before, and for hours you are still in seclusion, under the gentle touch of the breath of nature, accompanied only by the music of the singing birds, or the indescribable slush of dripping water or the cascading stream or waterfall? Have you been there before, in the midst of many but you are really alone, lost in concatenation, in the wild of destiny-leading soul-searching thoughts, where you look at everyone around but see more of the things in you than the people around you? Have you been there before where in your thoughts, you connect the little pieces of hobbies you manifested as a kid to the passion you discover you have as an adult and the challenges you keep seeing around you, and these little things just make up to much? Have you been there? Meditation takes you there.

> *Meditate on these things; give yourself wholly to them; that*
> *thy profiting may appear to all.* (I Tim 4:15. KJV)

The ESV puts it as:

> *Practice these things, immerse yourself in them...*

Think about what you are thinking about if it's worth thinking about. Life's purpose can be known. Meditate on your life's purpose. Meditation is a purpose GPS, you'll have to learn to use it.

MENTORSHIP

According to Wikipedia.com, Mentorship is a personal developmental relationship in which a more experienced or more knowledgeable person helps to guide a less experienced or less knowledgeable person. The mentor may be older or younger, but have a certain area of expertise. Forbes. com shares similar thoughts as Wikipedia and adds that the mentor is a professional in the same field who offers career guidance, advice, and assistance from a real world point-of-view. A mentor is another name for a teacher.

Whatever you are seeking to become, whoever you are pursuing to become, wherever you are hoping to go, someone's been before. They may not have been in the form and fashion that you are planning, but they have some experience having been there before you, and they could help with that.

Talking from the perspective of a business coach, I would rather that a starter in business gets to learn in a mentoring fashion as he or she starts out than get an MBA. Take nothing away from the prestige and advantages that an MBA gives, but there are more to gain from business mentoring no matter how informal it may appear. As a life and personal development coach, I would offer same suggestion to everyone who wants to grow.

Everyone who gets mentored gets to stand on the shoulder of the mentor and see farther into the future. Such persons are more likely to get better and faster results than others because they learn from those who've been there before. A mentor helps you navigate the waters of your areas of interest.

A mentor helps you find your purpose in life.

A good mentor sees something in you that you could never see for yourself. Something that's always been in you; something you couldn't really separate from the mere hobby of a child; the mentor engages the eye of experience to see what your eye of interest cannot see. A mentor encourages you to do more of one thing than another because he or she believes you could achieve better success with that thing instead of the other. The mentor helps you to direct your focus even if it is quite tough for you to see what he's seeing or understand what he's saying.

A good mentor helps you nurture what you have that you may not even know you have.

You can have several mentors to cover the several areas of your interest. Someone who speaks, writes and is an entrepreneur as well, might have different mentors to guide him in all these various areas. Even if you do not have diversified fields, what stops you from having to see the same thing from the different perspectives of different mentors and learn all that you can from all of them, so you can build on that? Most of us are already doing that. That's why we read different books by different authors and listen to as many as we can or even maintain a personal relationship with all of them.

Truth is, in some cases, you may not even have a personal one-on-one relationship with someone you call a mentor. Although it's always better to have such relationships. Your contact with the person might just be through tapes, books, seminars, mails, etc, but the person's words just have an influence on you, and they help to press your "reset" button as often as you encounter them.

Charles William Eliot seems to agree with this. He said: "Books are the quietest and most constant of friends; they are the most accessible and wisest of counselors, and the most patient of teachers." Alexander the Great, whose teacher was Aristotle once quipped that "I am indebted to my father for living, but to my teacher for living well." The assignment of a mentor in your life's journey is difficult to quantify. You can't really tell how much you owe your teacher.

Most people want someone who can guide them in the discovery and fulfillment of their life's purpose, but they do not know how to enter into, and service that relationship. It comes in various ways I must admit, and the most lasting of these, I have seen, come almost informally. You first have to identify the person whom you want to call a mentor. You must have the same beliefs. He must have attained some level of success in his profession, has values that you cherish and symbolize success in some ways. I do not mean one who has all the flashy things on which people place emphasis today. Success is relative, though, but you must find someone who above all, has the right spirit – the spirit that pushes through to success, that person makes a good mentor.

You may have to walk up to the identified person, and ask to be a protégé, or just warm your way up to the person somehow, and make yourself useful to the person. I doubt if anyone would really want to reject you learning from them, though, but even if it appears so, your courteous insistence will pay off eventually. It is a bigger blessing if the mentor is the one that identifies you, and beckons you to follow like it was for the Disciples of Christ. At such opportunities, get the maximum lessons of life you can get.

When you find a mentor, do not be as interested in what financial or material things you get from him as you should be with the teacher-student relationship that took you to him to start with. Never get to ask for money from your mentor. If he chooses to give you, or gets to know of your problems and offers to help, that's different, you may accept. Getting a book from a mentor is more important than getting a shoe, and his contact more than a car. The lessons he'll teach you are invaluable, don't destroy the privilege with greed. A good mentor knows just what is right for you, and what lessons you should be learning at what time. Once you get to ask for a financial or material favor from him, you close the door to the greater blessings that may abound in that relationship.

As you progress with him, find opportunities to reach out to him with gifts. Most mentees think their mentors have enough and do not need anything from them. Sure they may have more than you, and it is not your gifts they are waiting for, but, don't forget that the gifts of a man makes room for him, and brings him before great men, and not mere men, as the wisest man that ever lived once said. Your gifts make you more endearing to him, and in turn, he'll want to do more to help you. Accord your mentor maximum respect, it is a seed you are sowing that will come back to you, and when he gives you directions, be open to following them. As you service this relationship, you will find that you are being led into your dream.

TIME

Time shall tell.

Those three words probably rank among the most used expressions of all time. Time just has a way of making things known. Year after year, archeologists keep digging out artifacts to prove or disprove, confirm or discard a belief or something. Just before the commencement of the writing of this book, it was a finding at the foothills of the Judean Mountain west of Jerusalem, the skull of Goliath. That giant skeleton of a giant was unearthed. The slingshot David fired into his head was still intact, and the finding also went far to confirm that the man indeed stood at some ten feet in height. Time revealed that the bible story is not a fable after all. Time revealed that.

What do you think your purpose in life is? Time shall tell.

Time will always keep things for you that are meant for you – in your heart. No matter how carried away you become by other activities that you get yourself into, your main purpose may take a back seat in the interval but it never goes away. It always comes back. Somewhere, in the very recess of your heart, there your purpose is lurking, waiting for you to come back to it. If you can find that, after all these years, your passion for a purpose task you felt you should have done remains undiminished, then you ought to give it a shot. Purpose never dies. Time always reveals it.

Sometimes, the only thing you could really do is to wait for the fullness of time when that purpose will find expression. This is what I mean. Life happens to us in stages. Things will unfold in years as you go through life. No matter your agitation and aspiration, you cannot bring to pass now in your life what has been designed to come in the next twenty years. He makes all things beautiful in His time, and time and chance happen to them all. So says the good book. In fact, the tribe of Issachar was praised as the people who understood time and seasons. Brother, there is time for everything.

This knowledge just kind of helps you know that beyond you, there is a God who rules in the affairs of men, and beyond you, there is a design by which life must run.

You just got to wait for your time. It is in not wanting to do this that a lot of people run themselves into irreparable but avoidable errors of life. They dip their hands into things they shouldn't, and join with people they shouldn't, and they just get their lives messed up. Most of these things happen when we start comparing ourselves with others. We are not them, and they are not us. When someone is at a certainly enviable level in their lives, rejoice with them, and expect that your own day will come when people will rejoice with you too. You have need of patience after you have done all you can, including prayers. You need to start waiting expectantly after all those. The answer to your prayers may have been granted, and in the next five years, it is guaranteed. That is the time for the manifestation. You cannot hamstring God to bring it now. There is time for everything.

Your purpose has a time for full blossoming, as you work at discovering it, you must do all you can to become it, but you must give it time to have full expression. This all reminds me of the story of the caterpillar in the cocoon.

Someone walking along a pathway found a caterpillar that was struggling to come out of a cocoon. By the way, the caterpillar is a butterfly in the making, and the cocoon is the home where it matures. And by design, the caterpillar must go through a process of life to appear a butterfly. This man watched for a while, and thought, he needed to help this caterpillar come out earlier to save it the whole struggle. He got his knife and split the cocoon open and was amazed at what he saw. The caterpillar's part that had come out through its own struggle was the only part that was formed, the remaining part in the cocoon were yet forming and the man had scuttled the growth when he elected to help. If he left the caterpillar with its struggles, it will eventually come out a well-formed and beautiful butterfly. That is the case with most of us who want to hurry things in life. In scuttling our struggles, we destroy our purpose. There is time for everything, and in the process of time, the fullness of your purpose will manifest. Go through it, don't scuttle it.

INTUITION

This could also be called instinct. The Encarta dictionaries defined it as a strong natural impulse: powerful impulse that feels natural rather than reasoned. It is also defined as a knack: a natural gift or skill.

In the Yoruba parlance, this natural gift, impulse or feeling is what is referred to as the charm of the elders. It is their ability to know things will happen and forewarn others about it. It's weird, though, but when you ask how they knew, they do not have a particular direct answer. Sometimes they just say, "I just felt it". No better explanation. Whatever generates that kind of feeling.

Sometimes, the only reason you are going in one direction rather than another, doing one thing instead of another is not even something you can explain. You are short for words on reasons, but you just know that what you are doing is better. Sometimes you just feel something is going to happen, and without fail, that thing happens, and you say to yourself, "I saw that coming". Should anyone ask how, I doubt if you'll have a better answer than, "I just knew in my mind". That is intuition at work.

We need to pay attention to intuition.

On the other hand, there is always a still, very small voice on the inside that says 'okay' albeit quietly. It says 'good job' by giving you peace and rest. It sounds 'click' albeit inaudibly. It sends a smile across your face when you have achieved some feat no matter how small or huge especially when the only reason you undertook the task was because you just felt like it, not because you were sure of the outcome. It makes you want to hug the next person as a result of 'feeling good'.

Intuition speaks. Intuition guides. Intuition directs.

You may not have recognized the voice, feeling or emotion of intuition yet because you have not processed your intuition enough. You have not taken enough time to understand how intuition guides you but I can guarantee that you have at one point in time or another listened to your inner self and responded by doing what it felt like doing, and you felt better after doing so because you got your expected results.

It is that better feeling I am asking you to reinforce. Whatever you do consistently, you get better at. Just by doing something over and over again, you improve your performance rating on it. Same goes for listening to and following your intuition. The more you follow, the better you get at following until it becomes a way of life just like eating, sleeping and working.

Sometimes in our lives, we are in situations where every other person seems to be saying something but deep in our hearts, what we are hearing is ways apart from what everyone is saying. Though we cannot place a finger on it, we just feel convinced to follow our hearts rather than the 'wise counsel' everyone seems to be giving us. In such times, sometimes, when we follow our heart, we get our best results in life.

You need to set time aside to ponder when you are at crossroads about any decision you want to make and go at it by the way of intuition. Ask yourself why you want to do it in a particular way instead of another way, or why you are choosing the one over the other. In doing that as sincerely as you can possibly be to yourself, you separate superficiality from purpose-driven good.

Take an example of someone who is in a quandary about which job to take among two opportunities he or she has. And another example of someone who is confused about which to become: an entrepreneur or work in a paid employment.

In the first case, it is easier for the concerned person to look first at the pay check that comes in at the end of the month from each job than to look at the opportunities for personal growth that the job offers. If the main reason for getting that job is the income it guarantees (which almost always is the case), you will soon need another reason to stay in that job. If salary is the main reason for the job, you will not notice the other things that will be denied you in the job because you are beclouded by the higher pay. That reason is the superficial one. A greater reason is the growth potential in the job, and I cannot possibly remember how many people I've counseled with, who would readily give up their higher paying jobs for a lower paying one with more value-adding benefits to them. The same value-adding reasons go for the second instance – entrepreneurship versus paid employment. You must separate between superficial and value-adding reasons, and never let the superficial reason for getting into something become more prominent than value-adding reasons. To generate the value-adding reasons which come by intuition, by the way, you need to set time aside and work your mind through why you really should pick one over the other.

CIRCUMSTANCES

I once watched and paid attention to a blind fellow who was reading from his braille. The way he was guided through the letters with his fingers was something outside my realm of understanding. His fingers groped and his mouth pronounced the words. It was more like his mind was his eye. Watching him brings the image of someone in the dark to my mind. It does some good to close the eyes when you are in gross darkness and just grope through. At that time, the only eye open is the eye of the mind, and that just about gets you through.

The experience of the blind whose fingers guide his mind and that of someone walking through the dark whose mind's eye is more effective than his physical eyes is sometimes synonymous to our experience going through life. We just grope our way through. We almost could conclude that circumstances are orchestrated and planted our way to guide us. We make our inferences from our circumstances in life. We walk the path of life from one kind of experience to another, and they are so linked that we find ourselves walking in the corridors of our purpose.

But we must know whether God is the One that orchestrated those events of our life or man has a hand in it or there is interference from the devil. To do this we will need the services of the other purpose GPS.

The kind of incidences I refer to here are definitely not the ones contrived by man or the devil, they are the God-incidences. He just makes one thing come after another for us, and they are purely calculated to lead us to our places of fulfillment in life. Sometimes these experiences are a string of happenstances, some other times, they are largely unconnected events, but, they still lead to one's ultimate purpose in life.

Some of the incidences bring us sweet experiences, some bitter, some bitter-sweet. As far as it is God-ordained, it will be for our good. Sometimes we understand why we are going through, some other times we are just wondering, but they don't just happen without a purpose.

We may need to pay more attention to ourselves. What events have characterized our lives? What experiences have we been or are we more prone to? What circumstances have we most times found ourselves in? They may be well linked that we could easily read between the lines as if our eyes are widely open or they may be totally unconnected that we may have to walk through with our fingers helping us grope through as we see only with our mind's eye.

Joseph's is a classic case of circumstance-style purpose fulfillment. Even though he had dreamt that his entire family bowed to him - he was going to lead his brothers and indeed family someday, he had no idea how nor where that was going to happen. First, his brothers caught him and feigned his death to their father. Next, they sold him to Egypt. Next, his master's wife wanted him and his refusal landed him in prison. Next, an ex-inmate who had forgotten about him suddenly remembered and recommended him to the king. Next, the king made him a Special Adviser, and eventually saw no better to make the Prime Minister of Egypt. Next, he indeed led his entire family. What a string of events! Talk about circumstances.

Things happen in the lives of everyone which eventually lead to destiny definition for them.

Someone's daughter always loved to watch cartoon, and play with dolls, as is the custom with children. He soon found that his black girl had no black role model because all cartoon and doll characters were white. In trying to create a black character for his daughter, he found himself caught in the business of doll making and cartoon movies/television series creation. In another instance, someone loses a job dispatching certain kind of goods to distributors from the producer's warehouse. He soon thought to himself, wait a minute, why don't I just become a distributor or producer of this same product. He sought for and found help, few years down the line; he is in competition with his former employer. In another instance, someone loses their loved one to a particular kind of ailment or the deceased could not find help before death. In trying to make sure that fewer people die from the same ailment or that the same fate does not befall another person, the person takes it upon herself to find a cure or create help, and that becomes the purpose for which that person is alive. It may come in different shades and form, but never doubt that purpose can be discovered through circumstances of life.

Sometimes circumstances that lead to purpose discovery might not really come in the fashion described above. The sudden happening of an incidence in the lives of some people is what wakes them up to purpose discovery.

By the tragic loss of a benefactor, breadwinner, parent, guardian or loved one, a whole new chapter is opened for a lot of people. Suddenly they start to experience things they probably would never have if their benefactor were still alive. Some go through indescribable emotional pain, some through rough treatment in the hands of others, some through environmental change, many through complete overhauling of living experience. One main event, and then a whole new life, and discovery begins. Because they have to leave the environment where they used to be, and relocate to a new one, or because they are now exposed to a different kind of life from the one they once had, such people are pushed into what originally their lives' purpose is about. So, what appeared to be a terrible circumstance had a greater good in it after all.

Your experience in life might not follow the patterns described above, you might not even be able to create a direct link between one event and another, but when led by circumstances, it will nonetheless be that those coordinated or uncoordinated events lead to the fulfillment of purpose in your life.

9

Entering Into And Fulfilling Your Purpose

It is easy to go through the motion always. Going through the same process and stuffs you've heard taught in workshops, seminars and even group talks on how you can overcome certain habits and become the real you, and the person you were really meant to be.

I have discovered that it is easier to ask someone else to tell you who you are and to live by what they said. Put it another way, it is easier to ask someone else, "So, what do you think I can do?" and whatever they say becomes a picture you are seeking to become even if it doesn't tally with your real purpose. We let others paint on the canvas of our lives the pictures they feel, and guess what? We would rather struggle through life hoping to become that picture. Most of us obviously do not believe enough in who we are that's why we prefer the security that someone else's effort provide than that which may come from our own if we dare to work at it. It is far easier to put our cross on others than to bear it ourselves. It is easier but far less productive. Someone might help along the way to point you in the right direction but you'll always have most of the road to travel by yourself.

Do you want to discover your purpose? Do you really want to know what you should be doing with your life? Do you really want to know whether you are doing what you were born to do? You have a bigger part of the job to do in discovering that.

It is possible you don't know who you are because you have not paid enough attention to who you have become. You probably don't know who you are because you have trusted more the judgment of others than the knowledge or intuition that you have. You do not know who you are because you have not separated the quest for self-discovery from the pursuit of daily living. You do not know who you are because you dread what your search might produce. You do not know who you are because you take external struggles more importantly than internal satisfaction. You do not know who you are because your focus is more on what you will get than on who you should become. You do not know who you are because you pay far less attention to the impact of your life on others and you think everything starts and ends with you. You do not know who you are because you are in a company of those who do not know who they are. You do not know who you are because you prefer to be someone else rather than to be yourself; you tried so much to become like that idol of yours that your own identity disappeared along the way. You need to pay attention to what you need to pay attention to. You need to embark on the quest for liberation from the hustle-bustle of the ever-beclouding daily living.

FINDING WHERE YOUR TALENT AND GIFTS ALIGN MORE WITH MEETING HUMAN NEEDS AROUND YOU

I believe that every gift, talent or ability we have, have been given to us, above all else, to make our lives and the lives of others better. We must get to that point where our talents and gifts are answers to questions. Every question that any man may ask has an answer in someone else's action or saying. I believe, like Aristotle, that purpose is reached where talents and gifts are meeting human needs.

There is no talent or gift that is useless. The owner has simply not found use for it. Once man takes it upon himself to deploy his gift, he will find that there is someone who has been hoping and praying to encounter such a gift. The challenge is, most times great gifts don't come in tetra pak. They don't come in designers' outfits so everyone can recognize them. For the sake of laziness, pride, or both, the gifted or talented does not take time to fine-tune his gift. He does not take time to fashion it out and hone the skill to attract people and meet arising needs. This makes the rather powerful gift unattractive and un-earning. This is very synonymous to the biblical expression that a lazy man finds game but does not roast it.

It is, as a matter of fact, the major risk factor with having abundance of raw gifts. An individual who is ideas-driven, who is always full of ideas may find it no loss if he/she sells or gives off the idea to someone else. The person might even think it is better to sell this idea off than do nothing about it anyway. The same goes for a nation or country that is hugely endowed with natural resources but has a people or a set of leaders who care nothing about what values they can make of those resources. They consider rather the immediate gains they'll make by selling off the resources in their crude form. And you know as well as I do that crude resources never weigh nearly as much as refined resources. An unrefined stone may never be valued as gold.

A story I once read comes to mind about some colonialists who came over to Africa centuries ago. And somewhere in Africa, they found little children playing with certain kind of stones, immediately they recognized those as precious stones, but to the children, it was just another shiny stone. The foreigners offered them candies for those stones. Poor children – the candies meant more to them. Same applies to people who take no conscious effort to refine what they've got but give it away for immediate gains. Yet in Africa, Nigeria, the most populous black nation on earth is a classic example of a truly blessed country; having abundance of natural resources lacking only abundance of genuine leadership that will lead the way in the transformation of those resources.

The country mines almost every kind of natural resource you may think of. Although there are no reliable statistics, an online channel, synterra.co estimates that there are about 5 billion tonnes reserve of iron ore in Nigeria, wikipedia.org estimates that there are at least 2 billion metric tonnes of coal in Nigeria, while another report by kpmg.com puts the bitumen estimate at over 32 billion barrels (doubling what obtains in Ondo state alone), limestone in the south-western region of the country alone is estimated to be well over 31 million tonnes, lead is said to be over 100,000 tonnes, zinc well over 80,000 tonnes, and the list is endless of the abundance of natural deposits in the country, even the human resources (beings) are well over 170 million people. According to onlinenigeria.com, there is a proven reserve of 260 trillion cubic feet of natural gas in Nigeria - a gas reserve that is triple the nation's crude oil resources.

But do you know what she does with the abundance of crude oil and indeed other resources? It sells the crude rather than refine them, and in turn, buys the refined oil from the countries it sells the crude to. Do you get it? The country generates crude oil, sells it to America for instance, and then, in turn, buys refined oil from America. You are probably wondering what is wrong with such a country! That syndrome is referred to as the lazy mind in the scriptures. The lazy man (hunter) catches game (wild animal) but does not roast (process) it. The lazy hunter would rather sell off the game and get whatever he can get immediately.

Sometimes it is as much a question of circumstance as it is the discovery of purpose. You never really know you could do some things until the situation presents itself. I have met several people who discovered purpose by discovering situations that required their gifts. And to think that you need situations to discover your purpose, I can guarantee that there are several situations around, some natural, others man-made that will require your gift. Meet people's needs and who knows, you just might get engrossed doing that and devote your entire life to such a worthy cause.

DOING IT BECAUSE YOU FEEL LIKE IT

I once heard a great man in Ghana once answered to questions thus:

Question: Sir, knowing that there are other private schools around, why did you start one?

Answer: Because I felt like it.

Question: Why did you start a church ministry?

Answer: Because I felt like it.

Can you beat that? You undertake to do something because the opportunity presents itself and because you feel the need, not necessarily because you had a divine vision to do so. Not taking anything away from divine direction, if all you are doing is waiting until you have a vision or dream before you undertake to do anything, then I might as well say there are elements of fear and doubt in you.

There is always a place for doing something until…, you know, occupying until the vision becomes clearer than at the beginning. There is always a place of venturing out in faith believing that what you are attempting in faith will produce amazing results.

You can at least attempt something because you do believe somehow that you might do that. Even if you cannot put a measure on your feeling, or cannot quantify how much faith you have, you could at least give vent to that thing in hope, and your hope, who knows, may become the deal sooner than you anticipated.

If a man acts like he knows where he is going, people will make way for him, a wise man once said. But if a man is perpetually unsure of what he wants to do, he will never do it. When you start out doing something in faith, along the way, it will become clearer to you how else to do that thing. It will become more obvious to you; steps you will take and strategies you will deploy to get the kind of results you desire. But how on earth will you learn when you refuse to start?

Fear deflates, and deters from making any meaningful move in life but where faith is around, fear flies out the window. Where fear is in command, impotence will be the army. You must be willing to take steps when there is green light. Most times, the steps you take in such circumstances lead to the ultimate discovery of purpose that you yearn for.

CAN YOU SAY WITH CERTAINTY THAT YOU ARE DOING WHAT YOU WERE BORN TO DO?

Steven Covey once challenged people to close their eyes as if in death, and imagine people at their funeral, "What can you hear each person say about you?" he quizzed. Can you envision your life ending now, and on your death bed, you are satisfied with what you have lived out your entire time on earth for? Because I tell you, at the end of life, nothing of all you have gathered, owned or possessed here on earth will mean anything half as much as the fulfillment of your purpose on earth. It is not something that everyone can see or understand like you do, but if you have fulfilled purpose, you will know it.

Purpose fulfillment is never accurately measured by other people's parameter or standard. Nobody can look at you and truly assess that you have fulfilled your time on earth. Of course, they will judge based on what they see, hear or feel. You only truly know if the void is still there or not. Purpose! Oh, how sweet to discover early and live to the fullness thereof.

You will find, as you begin to fulfill your purpose that:

1. It brings you untold joy.

    It is such joy that neither wealth nor material acquisition could ever bring. It is joy that is measured only by deep satisfaction comparable to the impact you see your kindness bring to the life of others. You know you could have things for yourself and enjoy all the good things of life, but the happiness that that brings you is nothing compared to the emotion you feel when you see a well of tears on someone's face because you showed them a little kindness and care. That kind of emotion is what you feel when you truly fulfill purpose, this time only towards yourself.

2. It brings joy to the life of others.

    By doing something that you are born to do, everyone who is destined to find joy in life through you finds it. Without knowing it, your good work has a multiplier effect. On most occasions, you may never even get to meet with most beneficiaries of your fulfilled purpose in life. It is not necessarily the size of what you do that brings joy, rather it is the purpose behind it. Without intentionally setting out to bring people joy, that's what happens, because naturally, their joy is fulfilled through you. And it is sweetly blessed when you can see, feel or hear how blessed people are because of what you have done or are doing.

3. It improves your life.

    There is no way you are fulfilling purpose and your life is not improved. If your life is not getting better, you had better check it; you might be on every other track except purpose'. Fulfilling purpose, as it were, is hardly personal, it is more about others. These could be family, friends, community or society. Once you embark on this journey of making life better for others, yours will naturally become better. What you make happen for others, you make happen for yourself, Zig Ziggler once posited.

4. You'll want to do more, and find better ways of doing it.

    Once the purpose trip is embarked on, you find yourself gravitating more towards the direction of your purpose. You wake up to a new day, a new assignment, craft a new vision, make new plans and simply enjoy new life. You never really want to stop. Even when discouraging moments show up, you will bounce back and love to do more of what you have always loved.

5. It brings praise to God.

    Purpose is not fulfilled outside of God. When what you do make people thank God for sending you their way, purpose is closely represented there. When what you are doing causes men to realize that God indeed must have sent you, that brings God praise. Your activities, job, or whatever it is that you do that implies purpose must carry this dimension in it.

There is no way your work is in sync with your purpose that you will not realize it. I mean, I am yet to meet a single person who is truly fulfilling purpose but does not know whether he is. We may not be using the same parameters to measure or examine ourselves. We may not base our conclusions on the same templates, but somehow, you will know that you know that you are doing the right thing. That is a place where joy meets satisfaction.

I've met people who want nothing more than what shelters, clothes and feeds them but want more of what may help them take care of people with fewer abilities. They will go any length to go find and rehabilitate one that they hear of, and wail uncontrollably if ever they lose any. I've met countless others who just cannot stand injustice. If they see injustice meted out to someone, then they have a job for that moment if not for the whole day. They will defend the maltreated and want nothing in return except that justice is served. There are couple others who lose track of time when they find themselves amidst children. There are many who can't watch things go bad. You might want to contest that and say no one wants things to go bad. I assure you there are people who don't mind, and even among those who mind, our degree of response to salvaging things or restoring order to situations is very different. I am talking of those who are naturally and characteristically prone to delivering things from damage. There are people whose inquisitive nature just leaves you wondering what the problem is. And so on.

So many people find joy in bringing happiness to others. I don't know how they do it, but they waste no time in creating scenes of happiness to reorder the mood or douse the tensed feelings of those around them. Yet others find joy in impacting knowledge to others whether they do it directly or not, they are naturally happier when others are learning. Others yet are creative with things. This is beyond child prodigy, it is purpose fulfillment. These people create things out of almost nothing.

It is all different strokes for different folks. That is the way we are created, and purpose is almost always wrapped in those things that we are born with.

I believe. I believe that in most cases, we fulfill purpose when we do those things we are naturally gifted to do. I know it is hugely debatable and there might be many questions asked about many things. Be that as it may, there are fewer worries about whether one is fulfilling purpose when one works within the confines of the discoveries that he/she has made concerning himself/herself.

DO YOU FEEL A CONNECTION?

Quite naturally, as I have observed, and in my interactions with people from all walks of life, most people whom I notice are quite obsessed with what they do and are enjoying it to the fullest, their intuition drew them to their purpose.

The things that we get attracted to in life most easily, those things are probably indicators of our purpose. Let me ask you this way, what do you do or want to do instinctively? What do you get drawn to, or respond to? That something outside of you is the deep that is calling out to the deep inside of you – that could be purpose calling.

Somehow, we get to see those things even when others don't see them, we get to react in a certain way to those things and see what isn't properly done when others are probably wondering, isn't this too perfect?

It is like something in you dragging you along to that place where your instinct is feeling nudged. Without knowing why exactly, you just realize that is what you want to do. I know someone who just cannot stand injustice. If he is anywhere and sees injustice meted out to someone, he doesn't need to know who is involved, nor invited into the matter, he naturally takes up the fight. And you know what? It is so easy for him to notice where injustice has taken place, even when every other person sees nothing wrong. He is a social activist and runs an NGO for social justice.

Some people can't stand a dirty environment; they almost instinctively devise a plan of dealing with the problem. Even if they are immediately incapable of doing something about the particular instance they face, they never let it go out of their minds so easily, they nurse the idea of the best way of dealing with the problem. Something connects them to the problem.

Sometimes the problems, nay, challenges around us, are indicators of our purpose. We tend to see more of those things and get all the more uncomfortable with them. We always want to do something about the problems. The way it works is comparable to the desires that we have. For instance, the day you rev up your desire about a particular kind of car, and love to own it, from that day, you will see more of that kind of car around you. I don't know if it is a mind-thing, but somehow, those things that we create a desire for, just show up around us more often. So it is with the challenges that we feel a connection to, and problems we are created to solve.

PURPOSE GOES TO WORK

The jobs that we do, the tasks we attend to every day of our lives and the various courses of life that we wake up to, are the coats or jackets that our purpose wear to work.

Our purpose finds itself broken down into works that we must do each day. And every day that we wake up to work, we either enhance or delay the fulfillment of our purpose.

You find that you enjoy every day of work Mondays – Fridays not necessarily because of the handsome pay you receive at the end of each month, week or day as the case may be, even though that is important. Not necessarily because you have to survive and you are happy because you now have something that keeps body and soul together, even though that too is very important. Not because of the opportunities that the job offers you, even though that is an essential factor. But above all of these, because you are fulfilled doing that job. It is a real struggle to get people to understand perfectly what fulfillment in whatever they do means especially if they have not been there before. That's because spoken languages don't fully capture the expression called fulfillment, it is truly difficult to express in words.

It is possible that your job does not pay you commensurate salaries to your input, only a few jobs do. That sure makes you unhappy and want to opt out, but, despite the inappropriate conditions of service you face, you are not out looking for just any other job. You are looking rather for that same work in another place, form or fashion. It is not the profession you are unhappy with, it is the environment. The purpose in you cries out for expression but the environment where you find yourself does not enhance the expression, so, that same purpose goes to work in another environment.

Sometimes it's not even about the environment of the job. It is purely innate self-dissatisfaction; a high feeling of discontent.

Purpose is like the ice that is locked up in the freezer. If removed and kept at high temperature, it will thaw. But the moment you return it to the same temperature that it was in before, it freezes again.

When dissatisfaction is very high on a job, it might not be unconnected with non-fulfillment of purpose on that job. This is beyond pay checks, titles or position. I mean it is possible to have a high-paying job with great conditions of service and growth potential, but yet dread every other Monday, and that, not because of a particular boss or any other thing directly related to the job. It is rather because there is a void in you that that job with all the paraphernalia of its offerings does not fill. There is a purpose seeking expression, and until you find that room for its expression, no matter how much you make, you will only leave the room more vacant. And don't even think about it. Do not think that if you have a higher paying job, you will fill that longing. No. You will only keep going from one higher pay to another hoping to quench the thirst in your heart with the paper in your wallet. It never works. Never. Even in old age, on death bed, purpose comes asking to be fulfilled.

Jobs are jackets that purpose wears to work, but it is far better you have a job that enhances the fulfillment of your purpose. That's all I'm trying to say.

Where your job does not align with your purpose, you have the following options:

- To go after the kind of job that enhances the fulfillment of your purpose and substitute what you have now for that one;

- To keep other jobs – the one to keep you going, the other to enhance the fulfillment of your purpose;

- To abandon the job thing altogether, and give the desired attention to your purpose.

PURPOSE SHOWS UP AT THE FALL OF LIFE

Suffice to add that, you could get really soaked up in your job, going through the motions day-in-day-out and thinking "well I'm doing good after all", I promise you that unfulfilled purpose is not really bothered by that, it haunts. At the fall of life, when one would feel that he has seen all that could be seen, and done all that could be done, purpose comes "knock, knock…I'm still waiting." That's what happened to Joshua whereupon at his death, God said to him: "Joshua, you are old and well-stricken in years but there are still many more lands to be conquered" and you'll wonder, what exactly has Joshua been doing? The voice of purpose is the sound of regrets or wishes you hear from the dying.

At the point of dying, as several researches and articles have shown, people have more regrets about the life they can no longer have than they would have admitted when they had the life. Some of the regrets of such people include:

1. I was not true to myself. I lived a lie. I lived pursuing things that I do not have use for now, and reaching standards people set for me.

2. I never pursued my dreams and aspirations. Dale Partridge believes this is the first regret of the dying. I think so too.

3. I wish I discovered my purpose in life much earlier.

4. I wish I made more time for my family and friends. I wish I had been a better husband to my wife and better father to my children.

5. I worked too much. I used my health to get wealth, and ended up spending the wealth to regain my health.

6. I wish I loved more. I wish I said it and acted it out to everyone around me.

7. Hate took too much from me. I regret not letting things go, and resolving conflicts as soon as they started instead of bottling it up, and seeking revenge.

8. I regret not helping people when I had the opportunity to. I wish I shared what I had with others and touch a lot of lives.

9. I wish I allowed myself to be happier, and enjoy silliness once in a while. I wish I hadn't taken life too seriously. I wish I had more fun.

10. I wish I thought about this old age much earlier, and worked towards it when I could.

Bronnie Ware, an Australian nurse who spent several years working in palliative care, caring for patients in the last twelve weeks of their lives seemed to agree with these in a book she wrote titled: *The Top Five Regrets of the Dying*. Abayomi Jegede in a very powerful article he wrote on www. lifehack.org also agreed with these.

Dale Partridge admonished that: "Our greatest fear should not be of failure, but of succeeding at things in life that don't really matter."

What choices are you making today that will make the fall of life the picture you have of it? Of you on the dying bed and your family surrounding you holding your hands in turns and you telling them stories of the things you have seen and are seeing, and praying for them, leaving them instructions and wrapping up from here below? Or of any other more beautiful ending you could come up with? This is made possible when the call of purpose is heeded on time before the fall comes.

HELPING CHILDREN DISCOVER PURPOSE

A child may be abundantly talented and have the ability to do almost anything and everything perfectly well. The parent of that kind of child will be stunned with helping to direct the child in the area of the gift that they most desire for the child or feel the child is best at. If you have a child that shows great talent in singing, dancing and playing of musical instruments as he or she does in Mathematics, Physics and unrelated Biology, Physiology and languages, I bet you'd be confused how to help the child rightly.

I bet you'd wonder more than once in a while what part you'd have to play in determining which exact direction your son or daughter is headed in life. You'd seek counsel, pray, study, observe and do everything you could possibly do to know the fate of that child. I bet also that very few parents will think of waiting until the child fully manifests as the first option. Most parents will rather preempt the child, and nothing is wrong with that, except that the child may turn out almost totally different from all your permutations.

It is not necessarily conclusive that the child's purpose is in the gifting where the child is relatively proficient. You might be in for a shocker when the child begins to grow and shows less desire and love for manifesting that gifting where you preempted him or her. It is not uncommon that the child grows up and veers almost completely off the track of the tendencies that were displayed at cradle. Question: How best then do you help to direct the course of your child's life? Do you exactly play a role in choosing who that child becomes?

There are probably as many schools of thought on this subject matter as are the number of parents with children.

I did check out a few of what other authors had to say, and this is what Samantha Cleaver, with huge reference to Damon's work on same theme, had to say in *The Purpose-Driven Kid: Helping your Child Find a Calling.* To help your child find his or her calling, she encouraged you as a parent to:

1. Model it for your kids: Breed a family that lives and breathes idealism and purpose. Talk to the kids about work and purpose, and let them know what these mean.

2. Encourage their interest: Ask what they are interested in, and help them pursue it; help them find service activities that will help them make a real difference.

3. Understand that they likely won't follow you: Parents can only get critical in supporting and encouraging purpose in their children, they cannot possibly force them to do as they desire.

4. Be patient: Keep pressing, be patient and persistent with them even if it appears they are shutting down on you for information that concerns their purpose. Don't stop pressing to know about it – patiently.

Sarah Lemp also postulated a few questions in *Helping Kids Discover their Talents and Gifts*, which helps us to learn from our own experience how to guide our children. She asks:

1. Take a look at your own life, what kind of things are you involved in now, that you also took delight in as a child?

2. What hurts or struggles did you face as a child that have allowed you to connect with someone you otherwise would not have connected with?

3. What skills did you learn as a child that you still use today?

4. What challenge did you overcome that you can help someone else through?

5. What lessons have you learned the hard way, that you can help someone else avoid?

The task of helping your child or ward discover their purpose might be the most important contribution you are making to their development in life. The sooner they know where they are going, the earlier they can get there. In addition to all the experts' submission as above, I'll like to add the following:

You must let your children explore themselves. No one excels at that more than children. You need no further example, just look at the kids you have at home and observe how many things they want to do or can really do. Helen Keller once opined that "all life is an adventure or it's nothing!" Give them room to self-explore, and avoid placing encumbrances on them as much as possible. Only guide to make sure what they are doing does not violate foundational tenets and principles and constitutes no hurt to other people or the society at large.

Let them grow with it. Let your children grow with the positive green light tendencies that to a large extent tell you, this is where I believe this child is headed in life. Your role? Observe, guide and help make resources available to them that will enhance their exploration.

Expose them to impactful experiences and watch as they become fascinated by any of the experiences they are exposed to. Take them out to places, sit with them to watch educational programs, listen to what they are more interested in talking about, and allow them to go out on excursion to places that could actually constitute a lead – to their destinies.

Help to nurture and narrow their interest. They cannot grow up to do everything for which they showed tendencies when they were younger. You can connect the dots; be observant and seek the help of insightful people to connect the dots of the greater number of similar things they do as against others that they stumble on once in a while. Those activities on which they show higher interests and are more committed to, you can then concentrate more on, to nurture them on.

Understand their temperaments and know which fields are likely related with such temperaments. This can go a long way to helping them out when they show elements of confusion.

Understand that you cannot do the job alone of guiding them to their purpose in life. Teachers in school, Sunday school teachers, and family members as well as other people they regard as mentors or leaders also influence them in variety of ways. Your job though is primary in guiding them.

The points shared here are in no way exhaustive. There are other more authoritative works on the psychology of children, and career counseling that would prove of immense benefits to you and your children. Please do not hesitate to study those as well. Nothing is too much to learn in leading your children to their ultimate attainments in life.

HELPING YOUTHS DISCOVER THEIR PURPOSE IN LIFE

You've probably seen one or more of those kinds of teens before. They are called exceptional, smart or gifted children. Without any form of formal training, they are able to come up with ingenious engineering designs of something. They are able to construct a plane that flies, a generating set that is powered by human urine, they are able to come up with a combination of fruits or crops that heal certain diseases almost instantly, they are able to pull a car apart, separating every part of the car, and couple them to the details without manual, they are able to sing with out-of-the-world vocal expression and composure, they are able to play multiple musical instruments quite naturally, they are able to start a business which in no time becomes the talk of town, they are able to write with such skill that one wonders for how long they have been doing this, and…the list is endless.

For such youths, in some advanced countries, once the tendency is discovered, they are taken to specialized academies where their talent is transformed into professional skill, but in most other countries, they are made to go through normal academic rigours learning subjects they will never need in their lifetime, and preparing only to pass school exams. Eventually, the enthusiasm that should have followed the flair is constantly suppressed and the child is constantly unhappy, unfulfilled, feeling inadequate (as he or she has to struggle like a fish out of water), and in extreme cases frustrated. The child goes through the length of time (some six years) of his secondary or high school engagement struggling so badly with some of the subjects. In many cases, such exceptional students may still end up becoming the best in their classes, but that's because they are naturally endowed not because they really enjoy what they are doing.

This might just be the challenge with the teenager you are raising right now. He constantly asks to change school, and in every other school, he still finds it difficult to find fun schooling. In order to not get you angry further, he keeps his dissatisfaction to himself. You can clearly see, it's a bigger problem.

Patty Leeper developed a program he called The Purpose Programme after he also saw the success of Damon's work with children. Cindy Donaldson wrote the following on Patty's purpose-building tactics for teens:

1. Help your child find the interests, qualities, characteristics and skills he or she brings to the world.

2. Reinforce to your teen the importance of finding the things they are passionate about.

3. Provide a practical, concrete reminder of what your teen loves by creating a vision board. On the vision board, you should have images, words, etc. that represent or means different things and lead towards different callings in life.

4. Ask others to review the vision boards independently and then brainstorm a list of ideas that relate to the words.

5. Offer on-going support and ideas to fuel the conversation and encourage your child and her friends to share in the discovery of each other's interest.

In my experience dealing with youths and young adults over the years, I have discovered that many do not know where they are headed until they get to their third or fourth years in the university, polytechnics, colleges or any other higher institution they find themselves. Only very few tend to know where they are headed before they get to that level, and a whole lot more just want a job by the time they are graduating from school, having little or no thought about purpose. Most of those in the last category described are those who have more issues with mid-life crisis (which has been sufficiently dealt with in a previous section in this book). The crisis is not limited to this group, though, but since they did not start early to think about purpose, they eventually start, albeit a little late, at mid-life.

The curse of lack of purpose discovery for youths is exacerbated at the level of studying in higher institutions. It starts first with the parents who fantasize having children study certain 'first-class' courses in school. For instance, the parents want their first child to study law, and thereby become a lawyer, the second child to study medicine, and thereby become a medical doctor, and the third one to study engineering so they can have an engineer in the family. In another instance, some parents want all their children to study same courses and end up in the same profession as them, so they can have a family of, say, accountants – where everyone is an accountant in the family, or law, so the family is a bench of jury. In yet some other instances, the parents want the child to study certain kind of courses so he or she can take over the family business. Where you have a father who is a medical doctor in private practice with own hospital, he wants his child to be a doctor too and take over from him. The list of influence goes on and on like that. To be fair to the child and say it plainly, in most of these cases, the parents are selfish.

You cannot choose a life for the child without understanding the natural 'fit' of the child. Like you do have your own calling, so does your child. Have you found out what the child's calling is? Did God tell you what the future of the child is? If the child loves what you do, and shows passion for it, that's great, and should be encouraged. But if the child shows tendencies and passion for something different from your preferences, please accept the fact that you are not Assistant God to determine such destinies. You don't want the child handing over the school certificate to you when he or she graduates because he or she went to school for you and not for himself or herself. You don't want to watch that child spend six years in the medical school only to end up a musician – appearing to have wasted your investment.

Countless are the cases of children we've heard of, who get to the final year of their university education, and drop out of school, not because they failed, or were rusticated from school, but they just couldn't afford one more day in class studying that course. It's up to their neck, and they are just sick and tired of being sick and tired of that course. We've heard of other cases where children graduate from school, and the gift they have for their parents is the certificate they graduated with because they studied that course only to please their parents not because they love it or are called to it. After that time, they go in search of their love.

Dear parent, your child can be a nerd having interest for computers only, theatre art practitioner, musician, radio or TV personality, business person, social welfare personality, social activist, religious leader, sportsman, photographer, teacher, caterer…whatever, against your desire, you only have to do your part prayerfully to ensure he or she is on track.

Granted, there are times when you know where the child must head in life by dint of spiritual insight, you must carefully and prayerfully guide the child towards that from cradle. The child must begin to see what you are seeing early enough, and guided towards it. If you try otherwise to force that desire on the child, you may lose the child. All of us avoid that like a plague.

Another curse is the academic course which the child is given to study in school. Let me explain. Most times, people end up studying courses other than the ones they applied for in school. For several reasons that may include not scoring enough marks in the school exams, restriction on the number of students that may be admitted in the department, political pressure/lobbying by powerful people to get their own candidates into those choice departments, etc, applicants are given other courses to study other than the ones they actually applied for. The students also elect to study those courses they are given because that may be the third time or more they have been trying to get admission into school. They just can't let that chance slip by, so, even if that's not what they truly desire, they will "just manage it" like it is said in Nigeria.

A lot become disinterested in the study along the way, and really want out. Or they may just continue for the sake of the certificate – at least they also will be said to have attended higher institution of learning. That is why it is very common in our society to find that someone studied mathematics and is working in a bank, someone studied language and is working as an attendant in an office, someone studied engineering and is working as a call agent with sales company, someone studied pharmacy and is in an unrelated department in a telecommunication company, you will find so many of these parallel relationships everywhere in our society today. Other than job scarcity, misdirected purpose is the second factor for this malady.

Considering all these, you will find that so much needs to be done to appropriately guide the youth in discovering and achieving their calling in life. The youth must know and follow his calling. He must follow through with unraveling the unique personality he or she has been created to be. It will take time and effort, but it is well worth the try.

THE TIMING OF PURPOSE

This is a follow-up to one of the Purpose Navigation Systems examined in chapter eight.

I would that we read the whole chapter of the book of Ecclesiastes chapter three. It seems this chapter of the bible is read more when there are funerals. If only we knew what wisdom is buried in that chapter by the wisest man that ever lived.

I have found that man, in his pursuit of fulfillment in life, is often carried away by his cravings, his desires, and choices. Man wants things done, he wants nature to respond to him just like he would snap his fingers, he forgets that there is a God that rules in the affairs of man. Man often forgets that the horse may be prepared against the day of battle but victory is of the Lord. Man forgets that it is not of him who wills, nor of him who runs, but it is of the Lord that shows mercy. Man does not know that the Holy One sits on high and laughs when He sees the plans in the heart of man.

The search of purpose in itself is fruitless if it is done outside of the Lord. There is no us without the One who made us. There is no understanding of who we are and why we are here without reference to the One who placed us here. No one knows more about the product than the manufacturer. A fruitful search does not preclude God. God must be at the heart of it if it must make meaning. That is just the way it has to be.

If we could, we would just speak things we wish, and they appear; we would just desire things and they appear; we would just want things and they show up, but if it has to do with our purpose, there is a time for it – for its manifestation.

No matter how much you desire it, if it is not time for certain things to show up in your life, they will not show up. That is why it is needless to envy those whose time is now; it is needless to be jealous of those whose seasons have arrived to manifest. It is their time; there is nothing you, me or anyone can do about it. If what they have is of God, rejoice with them as you wait for yours. Some people fight this. They envy those whose time is now, they want to be like them, and they strive endlessly to find their own way of measuring up.

Rejoice with those whose time has come, in anticipation of your own time. Life is turn by turn like it is said in Nigeria. Thank God on their behalf, when your time comes too, people will do same for you. No one can possibly be so blessed that they take your blessings along with them. So refrain from envy and the appearance of it; your time will come too.

The time for the manifestation of your purpose will come. As you prepare, and play your part, allow God do His own too. *To everything there is a season and a time to every purpose under the heaven; ...for there is a time there for every purpose and every work.* What time is it? Is it time for the manifestation of your highest grace? Is it time for your flowers to be in full bloom? Is it time for the harvest of your seeds? Is it time for your showing forth? If you do not have understanding of time and season, you will always struggle thinking God is late in coming! He never comes too early, He never comes too late; He shows up just right on time.

Are you feeling you should have surpassed so and so level by now? Are you comparing yourself to someone your age that is doing far better? Or a colleague for whom things are just working? Sister, be encouraged. There is a time for that purpose. God sets the time, so you can't tell if it's late for you, or early for others. God owns the time, it is by Him that the clocks of our lives tick. In His time, He makes all things beautiful.

You don't have to despair; it is done in His time. When that time comes, it is in a hurry that you will forget whatever may have befallen you and has seemingly set you back; in no time, you will find yourself at the forefront with those who you thought have left you behind. In His time, when He makes, your showing forth will be evident to all. While you wait, keep at it. Keep doing what your hands find to do; keep fighting the good fight; keep enhancing your performance; keep enlarging your coast; keep improving; keep getting better at your best; keep it all up, when that time finally comes, you will be more than ready to manifest, and how lucky do you think people will say you are when opportunity meets you prepared? Think about it.

10

Destiny Beckons... Respond

Looking out through the open heavens of his balcony, his eyes caught this beautiful creature, a belle she's better described, taking a shower. Beholding a beauty is something only the mind understands. The eyes can see whatever it desires, but only the mind tells which sight is good for retention. And the sight of a beautifully- crafted naked lady in a shower with water slowly cascading from the very tip of her longest hair to the tiniest piece of her toenail; the indescribable master craft of the contours of her body making the passage of the water the eighth wonder of nature, such a sight the mind wants to retain I assure you. And to such a beckoning, hardly does a man say no, especially if that man is David – Solomon's father.

Sure enough, not all beckoning are so pleasant to the eyes. Some, maybe many, the eyes wishes it never saw, but the mind? No! The sight lurks in the mind somehow. Expunge it anyhow, try as hard as you may, few years down the line, a few months maybe, and the mind plays up the card again. Ah-ah! There it is, staring at your mind's eye, the sight you thought you deleted.

Maybe you should just consider it. The mind suggests.

He was doing just fine as an elderly gentleman in his father's harem, helping to tend the flock, and look over the family that he was preparing to lead in the very near future after his father's demise. A committed gentleman being the good son of his father, maybe as the custom demands of the firstborn son of the family; he had to make sure to continue the good heritage of Terah his father. But destiny would have none of that. Destiny would not be destroyed by a good custom.

What if you are told to leave the comfort you are used to, to a wild you have hardly heard of? What if you are told to "go to a land that I will show you"? Wherever is such a place? A bird in the hand is worth two in the wild, the saying goes, but as it concerns the fulfillment of purpose in life, you may as well let that bird in your hand fly away so you can gain a poultry you have no idea of. We cannot always understand what lies ahead of us. No. Sometimes we know, sometimes we just feel. Sometimes we both know and feel. Sometimes we don't know, we don't feel, we just want to do it, no explanations, no reasons. It is beyond us how these things operate, and rationalizing it is just doing a disservice to the ultimate purpose of our lives.

Like Abram, we all get called by destiny, but unlike Abram, most of us want to understand what is in that call before we respond, and that is good, but, that good stands in the way of great.

So desperate he was in the service of his Master. The kind of servant anyone would want any day. Frantically searching for where next service might take him – Asia, Bithynia, Troas, anywhere, he just wanted to do the Master's business. But destiny? Not in any of those places for him! It was somewhere else, someplace called Macedonia. Even if he needed a map to get there, it was the only place he could be that was pre-prepared for him by the One who sent him there. Obedient him; even in desperation, he knew listening for direction was indubitable.

If you always knew everything: what next to do, where next to go, what happens next, who next to be with, and every other next, you don't know enough. As a matter of fact, I'm afraid for you. Forgive me, but I think only self-delusional and people who don't know God claim to know all things. Please forgive my harshness; I didn't get the euphemistic expressions. You have to, nay, must get to that point in your life where you are asking: Where next now? What next to do? Who next to be with? And so on, every once in a while in your life. That's no sign of weakness. It is a sign that you know your life is beyond the comprehension of your little mind. Your life as is the whole world where you live is in the hands of the Creator of both you and the world. You couldn't possibly know better than Him.

The steps He wants us to take in life is one per time under His leadership. When you seek direction, you are growing, when you don't, you are stuck. Guess it's time to discard what you think you know already, and seek better knowledge. Your seeking is a growth sign, and a signal that you will find.

Like Paul, we all get to the points of desperation in our lives, where we want something, someone, and we want it, them badly. So badly.

They were newly- weds. Had dated for few years, and had become no- see, no- sleep friends. They were the perfect dates, a model to others, head over heels for each other, always holding hands, always posting pictures of fun times on the social media getting a thousand likes, and always getting positive comments and well-wishes from friends, and haters keep looking for points to throw shades at them, in vain. They could only end up together. They were made from heaven, and it was either them or no one. Or so everyone thought.

Outside, another man was seeing the lady. If she had a growing affection for him we did not know, but she was a master craftsman in the art of masking. How she masked her emotion and let the whole world see what they want to see, say what they want to say is beyond comprehension.

Few weeks after their wedding, at the climax of the honeymoon, she fell short of saying those words, but they were there, in her heart: "I'm sorry honey" maybe if she said it right away, they could possibly have found amicable solution, but she added the bomb, "I'm pregnant, but it's not for you." It was the loudest unsaid words of all time.

If you could catch up with the person who ruined your life that way and wrung your wife out of your hands, you would do to him what soap does to the eye, but it is the king, and the king takes what, who he wills.

That's just one of the many nonsenses that life rubs in our face sometimes. Life just comes up lemons sometimes; terrible enough to derail us from the path of life itself. And what more, he would not be allowed to live to see his belle - his Bathsheba return to him anymore. Maybe;

Maybe that's his fate, maybe that's what life has for him, maybe that's the call of destiny on him, maybe or maybe not.

Maybe someone just uses their position in life to take advantage of us and use us like they would. Maybe we have done all that good servants do in their workplaces. Maybe we are just unfortunate to be the one that suffered the fate, but things happen in life we cannot explain. Some lead to death, some allow us live. If you died, you won't be reading this book, but since you are alive, you are the one I wrote this book for.

Your job is undone.

I know you feel cheated. I know you don't deserve what life has served you. I know you have done nothing to be so punished. You are not even asking for too much, only that your Bathsheba be returned to you, and even that, life has denied you. You have prayed, fasted, mourned, wished, hoped, and if there is something you have not done, it is something you didn't know you could do. I know all that, God knows all that. That's why you have this.

It is time to get up again. It is time to pick up from where you left off. This is not the easiest thing to do right now, and it is easier advised than done, but you got to do it. The rest of your life depends on what you do, and whether you do it. There is a rising, a brightening ahead of you, only you can reach to it. You have circled this mountain of despair and sorrow long enough; it is time to move forward. Pick up the pieces of your life again. You have nothing to prove to anyone, you only have the call of destiny to respond to.

You are like the eaglet that was hatched among chicks. Ate with them, grew with them, played with them, lived like them, and was almost becoming them until an eagle flew over the poultry. Saw its kind among the brood, flew lower, flapped its wings over the poultry, connected with the eaglet, did that continuously until the eaglet's memory popped open to realize that this is not where it should be. It is supposed to be up there in the sky, reaching to heights that other birds only dream of, it flapped its wings, and flew after the eagle, vanished into destiny, banished into greatness. Look above you, there is that eagle flapping its wings over you, calling out for you, beckoning you, needing you to realize who you are, and daring you to become that person.

You cannot undo what has happened to you, but you can decide to move forward. You are not rich enough to buy back your yesterday, but you have the currency for your tomorrow in your determination. Destiny beckons, don't tie it down to the mess of the past. And in case you cannot get justice for the past you have suffered, Uriah couldn't, but God did.

David wished, years later that his eyes never saw what it saw. He prayed that God took the pain of his recklessness from him. He expunged the image from his eyes, but lo, not only was it lurking in his mind, his life was stuck with it. And the boy died. Fair punishment for a man after God's own heart – the greatest king in Israel.

THE SEARCH IS SPIRITUAL AND PERSONAL

The search for one's purpose is spiritual, very spiritual; and personal, very personal.

The approach of this book has been to create a balance between common sense approach to searching for real existence on earth, and spiritual perspective on one's mission on earth. No matter how we want to look at it, these two intertwine, and there is no physical without the spiritual.

If you don't pray to any God, don't seek any spiritual fulfillment, don't allude to any spiritual leaning or any of these things at all, there is only so little you may comprehend of the depth of life's meaning. There are finite understanding and explicable limitations on your rationality. There is not much anyone can do to help you know what you seek or find what you search for, because whoever hopes to help you, can only tap into the realm of spiritual depth to unravel the mysteries you seek understanding of. There is no earth without heaven.

It is not my job to argue what you should or shouldn't believe, who you should or shouldn't worship, I only want to make clear that there is no clear understanding of purpose if it is not spiritually pursued. That is why you will find that very many pages of this book are filled with pungent scriptural annotations; that indicates what I believe, who I worship and where I get my understanding of purpose. You'll have to choose yours. Everyone will have to choose theirs.

If you think you have been getting by without the involvement of the realm higher, it is not true. Whether you know it or not, the incidences of life that have come to define who you are, and where you are heading are not incidences after all. They are orchestrated by a greater realm. They are controlled by a greater force. Nothing just happens. You don't have to believe it. Your belief or not does not change the fact anyway, but the earlier you accept this reality the earlier you can key into it, and make the necessary tours in life with clearer understanding and certainty.

The search is personal.

The journey to personal fulfillment is, as it is called, personal. The love of parents for their children cannot make them travel the road for their children. Friends cannot take the place of friends on the trip. Teachers cannot take the place of students. Leaders cannot take the place of followers. There is no substitution. Everyone travels the road by themselves.

It is not necessary for people to determine how others will find and achieve purpose fulfillment in life. They really cannot do that. Everyone must define happiness the way they understand it, and define fulfillment the way they understand it too.

I have met people who walk in oil industries, getting huge pay at the end of the month but are unhappy, and I have met some who walk in private industries with very little income, yet do not want to close at the end of the day; they always look forward to another day at work. I have met school teachers who are definitions of satisfaction in life, and I have also met societal leaders who are manifestations of frustration. What is purpose for one is different from what is purpose for another. Not even the mundane and ephemeral things around us define it. It is personal. It is an individual thing. So stop. Stop comparing what you are created for to what someone else is created for. His life is his life, yours is yours.

Get on it, search for, and find your own purpose for living, and just live fulfilling it, what any other person does, is their business, not yours. Concentrate on your own business, and you will profit doing it.

YOU ARE SHOWN YOUR PURPOSE BUT YOU ARE THE ONE TO PURSUE THE FULFILLMENT OF IT

The path of life is twosome: someone leads you on, and you walk the path.

Through various means, we are directed towards a path (our purpose) in life, but we play the part of the pursuer to attain that purpose. There is no way one's purpose is fulfilled without the involvement of that person. No way. One who is meant to be a medical doctor must be ready to go to medical school to qualify as one. He cannot become a medical doctor just because he dreamt that he was attending to patients.

When a man does not play the part that he should play, purpose is unfulfilled. That does not negate what the man was created for. It takes readiness on the part of the man to fulfill in life. What you are going to get in life is in cooperation with what you demand to get from it. Are you ready to pursue what you have discovered you are created for? Are you ready to work towards the fulfillment of your purpose? Are you ready to put every other thing aside in pursuit of that dream? If you are, this is a guarantee: the One who made you for that dream has His hands held out already. You will take that hand, and you will be led on and you will fulfill.

PURPOSE PRESERVES

A man who is on purpose in life is preserved, and even if he dies, he dies fulfilling purpose. I have not read nor heard of anyone who is pursuing the purpose for which he is created that is not preserved in the course of that pursuit. The twenty-seven years that Nelson Mandela spent behind bars in the apartheid South Africa were enough to snuff the life out of him, but purpose preserved him because his work was not done. The many persecutions that Fela Anikulapo Kuti of Nigeria suffered in the hands of the many military rulers who would stop at nothing to make him stop singing, not many people go through half as much before they are forgotten, it was obviously beyond Fela's strength that he lived as long as he did, purpose played a part in it, because his work was not done. Like Fela, like Mandela, like Rosa Park, like Wole Soyinka, like TD Jakes, like Martin Luther King Jnr, like Samuel Akande Oladiran my father and all the likes too many to mention, purpose preserved them, and for those of them who are dead, there is no arguing that they died fulfilling purpose. A man on purpose does not die, because even if life is taken from him, his works live on.

And to add, this whole has nothing to do with age. The number of years spent on earth is just what it is called: number. What matters most is what is achieved within the period of time that is spent on earth, whether short or long. Some people live so long they outlive their relevance, but some people's impacts are never to be recovered from long after they are gone. Of such people, it would be safe to conclude that they truly lived.

STARTING OUT WITH SOMETHING, DOING SOMETHING ELSE ALONG THE LINE AND ENDING WITH SOMETHING ELSE IN LIFE

Someone had accosted me with the question that borders on how to describe situations where someone starts out in life with a defined purpose, but goes through life, and ends up finding passion for something else entirely, and the person used the story of Bill Gates who initially lived his life for computer software and is living for philanthropy now. "Can one's purpose change in his lifetime?" That was the question.

I believe everyone has defined, definite purpose for their creation. And like you must have read already in this book, sometimes there are derivatives of purpose that show up in life, some other times, interests show up to redefine purpose.

We must seek first of all to know whether the purpose for creation is being fulfilled. As it is with known names like Gates, so it is with the teacher in the village that no one in the city may ever hear about. Has he indeed impacted the lives that he is destined to impact? Can he own a farm, after he is satisfied with the teaching profession? Or even alongside the teaching profession? If you think yes, why not, then I'd say the same about Gates.

Besides, as we grow in life, our exposures will ignite certain interests in us, and our orientations about a lot of things will change. We will find for example that, money is not all that defines life after all, and that purpose is beyond all the glittering things life can offer. When you find that an entire village is threatened with an epidemic because they do not have clean drinking water, or you find that the same things that waste in your home like food could save some lives in some places, it will help you to rethink, and maybe you would also begin to share your little with the less privileged or use your wealth to eradicate polio in the world. And maybe that could redefine your understanding of purpose entirely.

Also, we must realize that the concept of purpose is, as has been emphasized in this book, directed by God the creator. If He guides our lives, sure He leads in the way we must go per time. When He says it's time to move on, so be it. We just move on to the next assignment He has for us in life. Even without being so conscious of it, we just get to the next bend of life, and on and on it goes.

Is it then possible that one is fulfilling purpose doing more than one thing per time or switching jobs in a lifetime? Is it possible that one started out as a banker and now is a teacher but yet fulfilling purpose? Is it possible that one was a doctor and now a businessperson, and is yet on purpose?

The line of questions raised above is very common among a lot of people, and that is because many people limit the fulfillment of purpose to the kind of jobs that they do. That is not an absolute view or perspective of the subject matter. That is not also, in any way, to play down the very important part that our everyday jobs play in the enhancement of our purpose in life. Hear this:

A man's purpose may be in the job that he does, but his job is not his purpose. Your job is not your purpose. It is rather the fulfillment that comes to you as a result of doing that job, what happens to others as a result of that job, and how that in doing that job or in having done that job, people are able to give God glory for what you do or have done, that is your purpose.

You need to get this perspective. Your purpose might not even have anything, as it were, to do with the job you wake up every day to attend to. It could be in the other things that you do without paying as much attention as you do your daily job. It could be in the one-time event that destiny brings you up to, and you rose up to. Upon the fulfillment of that one task, ripples continue across the length and breadth of the society that your action affects, and your purpose is fulfilled. And usually, that purpose becomes your job. Have we not heard of people who only wrote one book or just a few in their lifetimes, and yet the world just cannot stop celebrating their lives? Or people who led societies in troubled times, but no one heard of them before the crisis, but after the crisis, their part is played?

Purpose cannot possibly be measured as we do food items, distance, clothing and so on. We never really can tell how much influence the supposed little actions that may happen to be our purpose have on others. We never really can measure that in lengths, breadths, meters, or other such man-made standards. No, never. The weight of our purpose is first on the scale of the One who assigned it to us, and the impact for others to feel and the fulfillment for us to enjoy. That's all.

And as it concerns doing more than one job, or switching jobs in the course of a lifetime, yes, of course, we can fulfill purpose doing that. I mean, how many of us really stay with one job all our lives anyway? Jobs are just vehicles for our purposes. If the vehicle you are in breaks down, or is not serving you well, you can switch vehicles right? And nobody hangs you for that. There are sure immense advantages with staying long in an industry, that though is not the focus of this book, but a lot depends on the individual involved here, and on the leadership of God.

PURPOSE, LUCK, AND DESTINY

People generally tend to give their own definition to the concept of luck. When someone hits a big break in their career, business or life, that kind of meets people's definition of luck. The person is said to be lucky. But success is not necessarily luck. Success is success.

I guess we could tell who would become lucky in life by looking at how people prepare for their tomorrow. While others are busy snoring on their beds of sleep, there goes someone burying their head in work making sure that things take their normal shape. While working hard may not necessarily mean success, it is an indication that the hard worker may become lucky.

Things may come to people when they least expect it. Breakthroughs come sometimes like jackpots, and there just might not be any kind of explanation for it except to say "he just got lucky". Except in such times when divinity superimposes humanity, luck is predictable, highly predictable. We must ask rather whether we are preparing to be lucky.

Destiny, as a concept has also been talked about in this book. It generally means fate, or what people believe to be their path in life. Some believe their fate in life is to suffer or to be ill-favored. You could never really blame them; their experience has become their life's story.

But we must know differently.

What people describe as suffering or the picture of suffering and shame portrayed by someone's life, serves a purpose sometimes beyond the realms of man's understanding. God may not have put the suffering on that person, He doesn't do that to us, but in that circumstance of life that we have found ourselves, there is a good that can come out. In that mess, there can be a message coming out. In that trial, there can be treasures coming out. In that pit, there may be a Prophet In Training. It is like Gordon MacDonald said: "The ill that He blesses is good, but unblest good is ill". The purpose of such experiences is more important than the pain of the experience itself.

One's destiny is his purpose in life. It is the reason the person is alive. And if one cannot yet find his purpose for living, he should not craft a definition for it on his own. Purpose, destiny is divine, and should at best be divinely defined.

GO ON, FULFILL

Everything written in this book is written for you. I do not imagine that you read this book, and you dropped it without following up with the determination to not only discover yourself but to also maximize your purpose for being here. I would not imagine that you did not make frantic efforts to live your true purpose. Please do not do that.

It is time my friend to fulfill purpose. It is time to uncover the veil of fate, and reveal the personality behind it. It is time to press the play button of life's music. It is time to dance; to throw caution to the winds and dance to the rhythm of life. It is time to be you. It is time to manifest. It is time to deny the world no further of the privileges of having you around. It is time to impact your world. It is time to live the dreams. It is time to make life more like a fairy tale. It is time to fulfill purpose.

There is no stopping you my brother, no stopping you my sister. If we look into the future and do not find your signature there, should we not ask you what happened? Having spent so much time in this book in search of your purpose, I hope you cooperate with God to find it. It is your time, go on, fulfill.

About The Author

Ola Barnabas is a multi-skilled Public speaker, Author, Business consultant, Trainer and Entrepreneur.

Ola speaks to several thousands of youths and adults every year in conferences, seminars, workshops, religious gatherings, schools, private companies, public corporations, etc. He is a regular feature on various radio stations. He is a direct mentor to several hundreds of youths in various parts of Nigeria. He runs Kiddies Mentoring Program where he is a role model to several children and guides them through transforming their talents into profitable skills.

He has helped to build several tens of businesses, and plays an active role in helping several people to find their calling and purpose for living. He is an award-winning writer with over eight books to his credit with titles including: The Onion-bulb Principle: Getting Everything you can out of Everything you have, Starting Your Own Business in Nigeria, Growing your Business, Managing your Business, Entrepreneurship and Financial Intelligence for Students, Fundamentals of Management and Administration, Focus On Business Management Elements, among others. He has several audio books and CDs as well to his name. He enjoys unusual communication grace and has more than ten years of experience under his belt.

You can reach Ola Barnabas at olabarnes@gmail.com. You can also follow him on facebook and twitter with same name. You can have Ola speak at your events. Please send your enquiries, invitations and messages to the mail as given above.

Printed in the United States
By Bookmasters